CRIMES OF THE TONGUE

ESSAYS AND STORIES

Alicia Gaspar de Alba

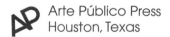

Arte Público Press
Houston, Texas

Crimes of the Tongue: Essays & Stories is published in part with support from the National Endowment for the Arts and the Alice Kleberg Reynolds Foundation. We are grateful for their support.

Recovering the past, creating the future

Arte Público Press
University of Houston
4902 Gulf Fwy, Bldg 19, Rm 100
Houston, Texas 77204-2004

Cover design by Mora Design
Cover art by Alma Lopez
MNESIC MYTHS by Alma Lopez @ 1999. Serigraph.
Used by permission of the artist

Cataloging-in-Publication (CIP) Data is available.

22 23 24   4 3 2 1

Para mis familias

CONTENTS

LIST OF FIGURES

Figure 12. *La entrada al cielo* by Liliana Wilson © 2005. Used by permission of the artist.

Figure 13. *El prisionero* by Liliana Wilson © 2004. Used by permission of the artist.

Figure 14. *Diablitos* by Liliana Wilson © 2005. Used by permission of the artist.

Figure 15. *Organic Barbed Wire* by Liliana Wilson © 1994. Used by permission of the artist.

Figure 16. *El ridículo* by Liliana Wilson © 2005. Used by permission of the artist.

Figure 17. *Mujer desesperada* by Liliana Wilson © 1999. Used by permission of the artist.

Figure 18. *Muerte en la frontera* by Liliana Wilson © 2007. Used by permission of the artist.

Figure 19. *The Wedding* by Liliana Wilson © 1995. Used by permission of the artist.

Figure 20. *La llegada* by Liliana Wilson © 1997. Used by permission of the artist.

Figure 21. *La caída del ángel* by Liliana Wilson © 2004. Used by permission of the artist.

Figure 22. *Girl and Red Fish* by Liliana Wilson © 1994. Used by permission of the artist.

Figure 23. *La junta de gobierno* by Liliana Wilson © 1995. Used by permission of the artist.

Figure 24. *The Successful Family* by Liliana Wilson © 1999. Used by permission of the artist.

Figure 25. *Proposition 187* by Liliana Wilson © 1998. Used by permission of the artist. In the collection of Alicia Gaspar de Alba.

Figure 26. *Greed* by Liliana Wilson © 2003. Used by permission of the artist.

Figure 27. *Sábila sagrada* by Liliana Wilson © 2008. Used by permission of the artist.

Figure 28. *La bella durmiente* by Liliana Wilson © 2004. Used by permission of the artist.

Figure 29. *El color de la esperanza* by Liliana Wilson ©1987. Used by permission of the artist.

1
CRIMES OF THE TONGUE, OR, A MALINCHE TREE INSIDE ME

The first time I heard the word *malinchista*, I was in grade school in El Paso, Texas, circa 1968. My brother and I were not allowed to speak English at home, out of respect for my Spanish-only-speaking grandmother, but we often forgot the rule, and sometimes, we forgot the even bigger rule, never to mix the two languages.

"You two are turning into *pochos*," my grandmother groused.

"What's a *pocho*?" I wanted to know.

"A Mexican who betrays Mexico by forgetting their Spanish," one of my uncles interjected, "just like those *malinchistas* from El Segundo Barrio who feel like they're so American when they have a big *penca* stuck on their forehead."

From what I could tell, being a *malinchista* was a bad thing, although I had no idea what it meant or that it referred to La Malinche, whom I would not learn about until a decade later in college. I was more intrigued by the fact that being a *pocho* (or *pocha*, in my case) meant forgetting my Spanish, which apparently the folks living in the tenements of the Second Ward were doing, even though, according to my uncle, they had a "cactus *nopal en la frente*." Having a metaphorical cactus growing out of your skull means you are Mexican to the bone. With this logic, *pochos* like those who lived in El Segundo Barrio were Mexican

1

to the bone and yet they didn't speak Spanish and pretended to be gringos; hence, they were traitors to Mexico. Somewhere in my confused subconscious, I gathered that betrayal to Mexico meant betrayal to the family, and it was something I was always in peril of doing if I forgot my Spanish.

We didn't live in the tenements of El Segundo Barrio or Chihuahuita, but in a little corner house at the intersection of Barcelona and Edna Streets in the Clardy Fox neighborhood, a short drive from El Segundo Barrio and the Coliseum, and only a few blocks north of the Rio Grande itself. Our neighborhood was mostly Mexican or Mexican American and most of our neighbors, like my family, spoke only Spanish at home. All the Masses held at Lily of the Valley Church were in Spanish, even though the priest allowed us to confess in English, if we had no other recourse to cleansing our souls in the confessional.

I was the oldest grandchild, but since I was being raised by my dad's parents after my parents divorced, I was also the youngest kid. I was born in El Paso, unlike my dad or his brothers and sisters, or my grandparents, who were all born in Mexico, and yet, I was as Mexican as they were. At least, that's what I was taught: that we were Mexicans, that we spoke Spanish and respected our traditions, and that we would never eat TV dinners or meatloaf. Never mind that my grandfather's favorite restaurant was Luby's, his favorite breakfast Corn Flakes, his favorite dessert, Jell-O, and his favorite treat, shared only with me, his partner in late-night-binge-snacking crimes, Oreos dipped in cold milk.

The disdain my grandmother had for American food was as strong as her contempt for *pochos*. For my own good, my grandmother often warned me, I better never forget how to speak Spanish. To make sure I never succumbed to that *pocha* fate, an inevitability that she tried to stave off as long as I lived under her roof, she had me copy out a page of *La Santa Biblia* every day after I'd finished my homework. Somehow, forgetting my Spanish was not just a sign of extreme treachery, but also, and definitely much worse, disloyalty to the family, my grandmother in particular who knew no English. Little did I realize that, for as wrong and prejudicial as their logic was, my family was also teaching me to resist linguistic assimilation.

"Are you a *malinchista* if you were born in El Paso, Texas?" I asked.

"You can't be a *malinchista* if you're a Mexican and don't forget your Spanish," my grandfather clarified behind his newspaper.

So, it was possible for me to become a *malinchista* and betray Mexico by turning into a *pocha*. I remember looking up "malinchista" in my grandfather's Larousse Spanish dictionary, but the word wasn't there. I turned to the section on proper names, but all I found was Malinche, the name of a volcano between two states in Mexico. A second entry said, "see Marina." Under Marina o Malinche, it said (and I translate): *Mexican Indian, died around 1530. She was the interpreter, advisor, and lover of Hernán Cortés, with whom she had a son: Martín Cortés.* Having attended only Catholic English-only schools in El Paso, I knew nothing about the Spanish Conquest. What did any of this have to do with being a *pocha*? I had gone as far as my young mind could go in solving this ontological mystery.

It would not be until I took a Chicano Literature class as part of my English major in college, that I learned the lowdown on La Malinche, or rather, Malinal Tenepal, and the indigenous history of the Mexican nation that would provide me with the context I needed to understand the life and motivations of this historical icon of my culture. I learned that the Aztecs, who called themselves Mexica, were descendants of the great Toltec and the Olmec civilizations. That they were poets and artists, gardeners and cooks, that they had libraries and schools, armies and aviaries, temples, roads, aqueducts and ball games. That they were very much a patriarchal culture, ruled by Huitzilopochtli, the God of War, and they lorded over the neighboring tribes, exacting tributes of food and flowers and human hearts. They were a class-stratified society (despite the fact that inheritance among the nobility was passed down matrilineally) and maintained a strict separation between the five social classes and the two sexes. Unless women were in the noble class, they were not allowed an education; their labor was physical and sexual. Malinal Tenepal was born into the noble class and was in line to inherit her mother's property and title, until her mother gave birth to her half-brother (not long after Malinal's father's death), and it was decided that the son rather than the daughter should be the rightful heir. Scholars estimate that Malinal Tenepal was between the ages of 8 and 12 when her half-brother was born and she was subsequently sold into slavery by her own mother, who later concocted a funeral for her "dead" daughter. The Mayan merchants who purchased her then sold the girl to the Tabascans and it was among the Tabascans that she learned the Mayan language of Chontal.

When Cortés made landfall in Yucatán in 1519 and promptly attacked the Mayan village of Potonchan, home of the Tabascans, the Tabascan cacique presented Cortés with a tribute of food, gold and women, and among the twenty female slaves gifted to the ruthless invader was the teenaged Malinal Tenepal, whom Cortés passed on to one of his captains. Upon landing in Mexica territory and finding his men surrounded by spear-wielding Mexica warriors far fiercer than any of the other tribes he had already vanquished, Cortés discovered that the slave girl Malinal Tenepal spoke two native languages and could translate between Chontal and Nahuatl. At first, there was another translator, a rescued priest named Gerónimo de Aguilar, who had been captured by the Maya years earlier; he spoke Chontal and Spanish. Malinche would translate for Aguilar from Nahuatl to Chontal, and Aguilar would translate for Cortés from Chontal to Spanish. But Malinche, with her innate skill for languages, learned Spanish in a short time, and Cortés had no more need of Aguilar as intermediary. Cortés had her baptized with the Christian name, Marina, and claimed her as his own. Time after time, in one deadly skirmish after another, Marina was able to intercede for the Spaniards and prevent their imminent death. It was because of her translation skills and her diplomacy that Mexicans (and non-feminist Chicanos) continue to see La Malinche as a traitor to her own people.

I credit Theresa Meléndez-Hayes, the professor of that Chicano Literature class, the one and only Chicana professor on the faculty of the English department, I might add, teaching the one and only Chicano Literature class offered at the University of Texas at El Paso (UTEP), with showing me my place in the genealogy of La Malinche and introducing me to my identity as a Chicana. This was 1979, so we did not yet have Cherríe Moraga or Gloria Anzaldúa on our syllabus, but we did have Antonia Castañeda, Tomás Ybarra-Frausto and Joseph Sommers's edited volume, *Literatura Chicana: texto y contexto*, which opened with a pre-Hispanic Nahuatl poem (translated into Spanish and English) as an epigraph commemorating the history, memory and renown of the ancient foremothers and forefathers whose stories would be told and retold to their progeny, those "who carry their blood and their color . . . the children of the Mexicas, the children of the Tenochcas . . ."[1] This epigraph connected me immediately with Chicano history, and with my mission as a writer, because, even though I wasn't or didn't yet consider myself a Chicana, I did call myself a writer, and I was one of those descendants of the ancient Mexican civilizations whose stories were my cultural legacy, which it was my responsibility to remember, record and communicate to future generations.

From *Literatura Chicana*, I learned that Mexicans were a product of the Spanish Conquest and that La Malinche was considered the symbolic foremother of the Mexican race, or rather, the mother of mestizaje. I learned about colonialism and *la raza cósmica* (the cosmic race), about *corridos* and the oral tradition, about the galvanizing power of the Chicano Movement and its solidarity with the farmworkers and the *braceros* of the United

States, with the revolutionary history of Mexico, and with the liberation movements taking place all over "Nuestra América" as José Martí called the continent of the Americas in 1891. Sor Juana Inés de la Cruz is in that book, as are Gabriela Mistral, Pablo Neruda, Gabriel García Márquez, Rubén Darío, Octavio Paz, Carlos Fuentes—all of whose names my grandfather and my uncles dropped in casual conversation at our Sunday family reunions. And there were other names that I was meeting for the first time—Américo Paredes, Alurista, Corky Gonzales, John Rechy, José Montoya, raulsalinas, Tino Villanueva—some of whom would later become mentors, colleagues and friends

Toward the end of *Literatura Chicana*, the editors include a short excerpt from Carlos Fuentes' theatrical depiction of the Spanish Conquest, *Todos los gatos son pardos* (1970).[2] Written in Malinche's perspective at the moment of the birth of her mestizo son from her union with Hernán Cortes, Malinche summons her child from within her body, calling him, lovingly, "hijito de la chingada" (little son of a raped mother) who is the "única herencia" "de Malinche, la puta" (only legacy of Malinche the whore) (305). Embedded in the words "whore" and "mother" is the common Mexicano view of Malinche as a traitor to her people, for her giving herself to the conqueror, her birthing the conqueror's child, constitutes what Sandra Messigner Cypess calls "the paradigmatic behavior called malinchismo."[3] La Malinche's relationship with Cortés and the use of her linguistic skills in favor of the conquerors becomes the primordial symbol of cultural betrayal that led to the defeat and conquest of the indigenous people. Thus, La Malinche converts into the scapegoat, the "figure chosen to bear the burden of [colonial] guilt" for her supposed complicity with the "malignant foreign interference" of the Spanish invaders" (Messinger Cypess 43). By stigmatizing La Malinche as the Mexican Eve, Mexico could blame the downfall of the mighty Aztec/Mexica empire on one indigenous woman rather than on the political and military exploits of both brown and white male supremacy. This scapegoating archetype has followed La Malinche since the birth of the Mexican nation in the 19th century— an interpretation shared by Mexicans and Chicanos until Chicana feminists started reinterpreting her life and revising her image in the 1970s.

The first Chicana revisionist history of Malinche is Adelaida Del Castillo's "Malintzin Tenepal: A Preliminary Look into a New Perspective" (1974), which methodically, through a close analysis of the historical records of the Spanish Conquest, and perusal of the primary and secondary sources that document the history of the Mexica, the Maya and the many other Indigenous peoples who occupied the land we now call Mexico, debunks the myth that Malinche was the Mexican Eve.[4]

> In effect, when Doña Marina is accused of being "una traidora a la patria," one wrongly assumes that there was a "patria" (similar to the *patrias* [or nation-states] of today). The fact is, there were many Indian nations within the Aztec Empire, and these nations were always attempting, through one rebellion or another, to regain their former independence. . . . It is willful to forget that the concept of Mexican nationalism (*la patria*) was introduced long after the conquest of México and not before. (Del Castillo 131)

In his essay, "Sons of La Malinche," Octavio Paz (before he became a Nobel laureate) forever vilified La Malinche in the Mexican mind by labeling her "la Chingada," the open, violated and enslaved Indigenous woman who gives birth to the mestizo/Mexican race, thus making all Mexicans the progeny of Malinche, otherwise categorized by Paz as "hijos de la Chingada" (sons of the violated woman), or progeny of a raped mother.[5] For Paz this is the shame that plagues the Mexican son and that accounts for Mexican nihilism. Instead of seeing the rapes of Malinche and all the other Native women as strategic maneuvers of the Conquest, Paz holds Malinche responsible, not only for her own dishonor, but also for the humiliation she passed on to her colonized offspring. Indeed, Paz's Malinche is a paradox: the passive "Fucked One" and the conspiratorial Traitor. On the one hand, Paz tells us, Malinche did not resist opening her legs to the foreigner, and instead gave herself voluntarily to the conquistador, like all the other "Indian women who were fascinated, violated or seduced by the Spaniards" (Paz 86). On the other hand, he interprets Malinche as the agent of mass destruction who used her language skills to betray the tactical secrets of the Aztecs and facilitate the fall of the great Mexica Empire. Because of these crimes of the tongue, "the Mexican people have not forgiven La Malinche for her betrayal" (Paz 86), he concludes.

For all the abject inertia that Paz saw in Malinche, she is depicted in the post-Conquest codices, namely the Lienzo de Tlaxcala and the Florentine Codex as a central figure or mediator between the conqueror and the conquered, standing either close to or pointing at Hernán Cortés, almost always larger than any other figure in the story. In Book XII of Fray Bernardino de Sahagún's *Historia general de las cosas de la nueva España* (General History of the Things of New Spain), she is described as an important figure dressed in regal clothing but is also depicted holding a shield, like those given to young boys of the Nahua nation to signify their role as warriors and protectors of their people. This is a clue to the respect accorded to Malinche by the Native people.

In "La Malinche: Feminist Prototype" (1980), Cordelia Candelaria argues that Malinche's nobility was recognized by the Indigenous people not only because of the way she carried herself, and the way she assumed her place as translator and mediator, but also because she spoke the elevated imperial language of the Tlatoani, the Emperor Moctezuma.[6] Tlatoani is a Nahuatl word that means "he who Speaks," and only the Emperor was allowed to speak to the gods, that is, the invaders. Moctezuma's dreamers and high priests had foretold of the return of Quetzalcoatl from the East on the same day the white strangers, traveling from the east on wind-drawn floating chariots (as the story was told), alighted in Mexico. The emperor fervently believed that Cortés and his company, in their armor and riding their majestic beasts, was indeed the god Quetzalcoatl fulfilling the prophecy. Since she not only spoke *to* the gods but also *for* them, Quetzalcoatl's human avatar, if you will, Malinche, became known as "The Tongue of the Gods" (La Lengua de los Dioses), and the Nahuas added the suffix *-tzin* to her name to signify her exalted position, making her Malintzin, for which Malinche is believed to be a Spanish mispronunciation.

The Spaniards, too, recognized Malintzin's greatness, not only as a translator but also as a diplomat who more than once had saved their lives, and so, they added Doña to her Spanish name. Cortés, of course, downplayed her importance in his letters to the King of Spain to apprise him of the progress of his colonizing mission, but Bernal Díaz del Castillo, who also accompanied Cortés, wrote admirably of her in his *Historia verdadera de la conquista de la Nueva España* (The Real History of the Conquest of New Spain) and unequivocally attributed the success of the Conquest to Doña Marina's linguistic interventions, without which the Spaniards could never have been able to bridge the two cultures.

In the last five centuries, how did this remarkable woman change from being the Great Speaker for the Gods to the Abject Betrayer of Her People? How did her value in Mexican (and by extension Chicanx) history transform from La Lengua to la Chingada? How did she, alone, cause the conquest, occupation and 300-year colonization of the colossal Mexica/Aztec nation? Did the Totonacs and the Tlaxcalans who allied with Cortés because they hated living under Mexica dominion have nothing to do with the overthrow of the Aztec empire? What about the pandemic of smallpox and other virulent diseases brought by the Spaniards that the native people had no immunity to and therefore died in droves because of their contact with the colonizer? Surely, these aspects weakened Aztec society and its ability to defend itself against the conquerors; Malinche herself died of smallpox within a decade of the conquest.

In that Chicano literature course I took in college, the early poetic interpretations we read by Lucha Corpi, Lorna Dee Cervantes, Angela de Hoyos, Inés Hernández-Ávila, Sylvia Gonzáles, Adaljiza Sosa Riddell, Carmen Tafolla, Alma Villanueva, Bernice Zamora humanized Malinche and spoke from her voice and perspective, as daughter, slave, lover and traitor's tongue.[7] They empathized with Malinche, I realized, because Chicanas, too, were given roles not of their own choosing and were expected to provide sexual and manual service to the revolution while the men running the revolution pushed aside their legitimate concerns as female bodies coming into their own empowered feminist consciousness. I marveled at how these writers braided their own prejudicial experiences within the Chicano Movement into their texts. As poets and activists invested in social justice, as daughters, wives and mothers who dared to question the limitations imposed on their female bodies by *la familia*—be that their biological families or *la familia* of El Movimiento, both led by the authority of El Gran Chingón, to invoke Octavio Paz—they embodied Malinche's struggle of resistance to enslavement and her subversive use of language to advocate for and reclaim their own rights. Here was a completely new interpretation of Malinche: the Chicana feminist Malinche, which I had to explore further in a research paper.

In 1981, Gloria Anzaldúa and Cherríe Moraga published *This Bridge Called My Back: Writings by Radical Women of Color* (Aunt Lute), that included two radical revisions of La Malinche: Norma Alarcón's "Chicana Feminist Literature: A Re-Vision Through Malintzin: Putting Flesh Back on the Object" and Moraga's "A Long Line of Vendidas," which she would include the following year in her first memoir, *Loving in the War Years: lo que nunca pasó por sus labios* (South End Press 1982). Anzaldúa, too, rewrote Malinche's story in *Borderlands/La Frontera: The New Mestiza* (Aunt Lute Press 1987), as did Ana Castillo in *Massacre of the Dreamers* (University of NM Press 1994). Alarcón wrote several pieces on Malinche, including her "Traddutora, Tradditora: A Paradigmatic Figure of Chicana Feminism"[8] in which she calls Malintzin the "monstrous double" of the Virgin of Guadalupe. While la Virgen symbolizes "transformative powers and sublime transcendence" and promises deliverance and liberation for every oppressed petitioner, Malinche "represents feminine subversion and treacherous victimization . . . and elicits a fascination entangled with loathing, suspicion, and sorrow" (61, 62). In the bulk of the essay, Alarcón performs a critical review of many of the Chicana feminist reinterpretations of La Malinche by the authors named above. Despite this revisionary work, Alarcón believes that as a "historical subject Malintzin remains shrouded in preternatural silence, and as object she continues to be on trial for speaking and bearing the enemy's children and continues to be a constant source of revision and appropriation—indeed, for articulating our modern and postmodern condition" (85).

All these Chicana feminist reframings of La Malinche destroyed the myth of the treacherous scapegoat for me and gave rise to my own inquiries and poetic reinterpretations of this complex historical figure. I wrote several poems about her that were included in my 1983 Master's Thesis, and, later, in *Beggar on the Córdoba Bridge*, my first full-length collection of poetry. "Malinchista, A Myth Revised," is a prose poem in five parts that summarizes the myth of Malinche's betrayal and her connection to La Llorona, the ghostly woman weeping for her lost children. The poem depicts several Malinches: as La Lengua/the Tongue of the white gods who could also speak the sacred language of the Tatloani Moctezuma; as the sexual slave of a bearded foreigner who raped her and penetrated her being with his conqueror's tongue; as the mother of the first mestizo son, who is born with the black eyes of his Indigenous mother and the curly hair of his Spanish father whose own supposedly pure blood was likely mixed with Moorish blood, the boy's skin color a "café-con-leche" mixture of both races. In the last two sections of the poem, Malinche's story interpolates *mestizaje* with border crossing. While mother and newborn sleep under the night sky, the mother exhausted from her labor, the boy already haunted by furtive dreams, a coyote lurks near the river, referencing either the predatory animal itself or the people who prey on those who cross the border without papers into the [un]Promised Land. The poem closes with Malinche transformed into La Llorona wailing at the border's riverbanks for her murdered child, not because she is sorry for a crime she did not commit, as the downfall of Tenochtitlan had already been prophesied in the Aztec calendar, whether or not she served as the conqueror's Tongue. Malinche/Llorona is screaming for revenge against Cortés for sacrificing her land and her people to their white god.[9]

In another poem from that collection, "Letters from a Bruja," I imagine what Malinche's mother might have said to her daughter about her decision to sell her into slavery.

> . . . you are conceived, hija,
> from the worm of incest.
> Already your seed bears the gift of darkness.
> Already your name washes up
> on the salty foam
> between my thighs: Malinal, Malintzin,
> brown woman of tongues and trickery.
> Malinche, mother of the new breed. (*Beggar on the Córdoba Bridge,* 46)

The incest theme crops up again in my short story in Spanish, "Los derechos de La Malinche,"[10] a story within a story that parallels the first-person narrator's rape by her father and Malinche's rape by Cortés. Unlike the outer frame story, in which the daughter has no control over the "daily bread" she gets from her "Papacito" (or as Paz would put it, being her father's "Chingada")—a secret that she has carried all her life and that has hardened in her throat like a tumor—Malinal Tenepal (the sold daughter who was dispossessed of her title and her inheritance) understands the inevitability of her fate as a slave and a woman. Summoning the strength of her goddesses, Tonantzín and Coatlicue,[11] Malintzin sets a trap for the conquistador with the thorny skin of a prickly pear. Doña Marina realizes that even at her most disgraced moment, she does, indeed, have some power to determine the outcome of her "baptism" into a colonized destiny.

In the frame story, the narrator's grandmother tries to justify the father's absence. It's not that he was a deadbeat, albeit handsome, alcoholic of a father; it's that he felt embittered by his daughter's abnormal choice of a life without a man. Hence, like Malinche who, according to Octavio Paz, "gave herself willingly to the conqueror," a sin that earned her the eternal blame of the Mexican people, the daughter gives herself willingly to another woman, and this act of lesbianism is the shameful betrayal that the father could never forgive and that drove him away from his daughter, away from all his obligations as a father; it was this indignity and unforgiveness that festered into alcoholism and led El Papacito to drink himself into an early grave at the age of fifty-two. *Mea culpa, mea culpa.*

Forty years later, I am still researching, teaching and writing about Malinche in my poetry and fiction, my classes and academic books. And I am far from alone. In fact, Malinal Tenepal continues to inspire a legion of reinterpretations. A quick perusal of Google Scholar or Academia.edu using the name Malinche in the search engine shows how many others in a variety of fields, publications and institutions both within and outside of the United States, in English, Spanish and other languages, are also rewriting Malinche or contextualizing her name and story in discourses beyond the Conquest. Obviously, her story resonates as much today as it did in the early days of the Chicano Movement, and that resonance multiplies in concentric rings as more and more scholars see her not as the passive "Chingada" (Fucked one) and symbol of the Conquest that Octavio Paz and Carlos Fuentes immortalized, but rather as a rape survivor and multilingual diplomat with her own historical agency.

Pilar Godayol argues in "Malintzin, Malinche, Doña Marina: Re-reading the Myth of the Treacherous Translator," her review of the literature on Malinche as both historical figure and cultural trope, that there are as many Malinches as there are multiple interpretations and translations of her life and myth.[12] It is because of this plasticity that Malinche, like her co-symbolic sisters, La Llorona and la Virgen de Guadalupe, can metamorphose into so many different meanings depending on the translator/interpreter. Malinche can be read as 1) the treacherous translator who used her power of language to reveal the tactical secrets of her people to the conquering foreigners and so brought down the Mexica/ Aztec empire; 2) the Mexica girl of noble birth who was sold by her own mother so that her brother from another father could inherit her title; 3) the willing mistress of Hernán Cortés, part of a harem given to the conquistador as tribute to whom the Mexica believed to be a reincarnated Quetzalcoatl; 4) the religious convert to Christianity who knew her survival and that of the Native people was tied to the faith of the conquerors; 5) La Chingada, the raped mother of the new mestizo race; or 6) as most Chicana feminists see her, the sexual slave of conquerors and soldiers, the betrayed daughter and reviled mother whose only treachery was rebelling against the patriarchal codes of her culture.

In *[Un]Framing the "Bad Woman": Sor Juana, Malinche, Coyolxauhqui and Other Rebels With a Cause* (UT Press 2014), I call Malinche one of the three primordial *mujeres malas*, or socially constructed "bad women," of our Mexican genealogy who show us, by example, what it means to decolonize our minds and rebel against patriarchy for our own sake and that of our future generations. What it means to reject not only colonization but also patriarchal exploitation of our minds and bodies. To be a *malinchista* means you *are* a traitor, after all, but what you betray are the sexist, heterosexist, homophobic and transphobic gender codes of Chicanismo. In other words, you use your mind, your tongue and your body in any way that you desire. This new *malinchista* cultivates her intellectual skills and linguistic talents not only for her own survival, as Malinal Tenepal did, but also, and perhaps more importantly, for self-empowerment and pleasure. Because Chicana lesbians "have become the latter-day Malinches of Chicano culture,"[13] it is necessary to unframe *malinchismo* and reframe it as a new mirror of Chicana resistance and affirmation.

In my poem "The Roads Out of the Body," from which I have taken the main title of this essay, Malinche represents this other kind of betrayal, lesbian love or the climbing into "the arms of another woman,/ a Malinche tree/ inside me" (*Beggar on the Bridge* 48). Here is another crime of the tongue. The Malinche tree is a play on the Judas tree, evoking the same sense of betrayal as the legendary tree from which Judas Iscariot is said to have hung himself in shame for having betrayed Jesus Christ. The narrator's lesbianism is a manifestation of a Malinche tree inside her, not a Judas tree whose dangling seedpods and blood-red blossoms are reminiscent of the self-lynched body of Christianity's primordial traitor. This is a redemptive tree whose roots reach back to Malinche to branch off, or separate, the notion of "women/and sins" (49). Loving ourselves is not a sin, saving ourselves is not a sin, nor is passion between women a sin. The "arms" that "crawl out wings" are the arms of a liberated being, no longer trapped in the cultural expectation of women as inherently sinful or shameful, who is free to express desire in the form that she finds most satisfying. *La Lengua* of the gods becomes the lover's tongue, and the language of betrayal is transformed into an orgasm between women. *"Quiero gritar*, she says/*Give me your tongue./Make me scream"* (48).

2
THE BORDER BEAT, 1921

Alberto Morales looked at his reflection in the plate-glass windows of *The El Paso Herald* and saw that his hat was crooked again. He straightened it, mumbling to himself that he couldn't touch his hat during the interview. He would lay it on his lap after shaking the man's hand firmly and being asked to take a seat. He would slide his hands under his thighs as he answered the man's questions, sitting straight and sure of himself and never looking down at his hat.

These had been his wife's instructions. It was she who had convinced him to apply.

You're an American citizen, she'd said. *You have a right to apply for any job you want. Here, put on your shirt. See how nice I starched it for you? Just remember to keep your hands off your hat, Albert. Sit on them if you have to. Stop acting like you're an alumni of the I Hate Myself Club in high school. You're more than qualified for this job.*

When Rosemary spoke to him like that, Alberto could almost feel the brown draining out of his skin, could almost imagine that his father was a conductor for the Southern Pacific instead of a day laborer who laid the track for it, and that his mother sold beauty products instead of burritos door to door to supplement her meager salary as a cleaning lady. Alberto could see his daughters growing up without fear or shame, nobody pitying them or laughing at their accents, nobody denying them a library card or a school placement or a job.

He straightened his hat again, wiped around his mouth and under his collar with the handkerchief Rosemary had embroidered with his initials, *AM*, and walked into the cool lobby of the *El Paso Herald* building shouldering the canvas rucksack he had used in school. *I scrubbed my knuckles raw trying to clean all the stains on that filthy bag, Albert,* Rosemary had said. *I don't want anybody calling you a dirty Mexican.*

"Excuse me, can I get an application, please?" he said to the young lady at the reception counter.

The receptionist looked confused.

"I want to apply for the job," Alberto said, burying his hands in his trouser pockets. "I read the advertisement in *The Herald.*"

"Bless your heart. Which position are you here for—reporter or circulation manager?"

"Reporter," he said, clearing his throat.

She told him to take a seat while she got her Super and disappeared behind a frosted glass door. Alberto walked around looking at the framed front pages that covered one wall of the reception area. It made his skin tingle to think that one of those stories could have his byline one day. He did not even have time to sit down before the receptionist returned, followed by a redheaded man in funny glasses.

The man strode up to Alberto with a baffled scowl. "Can I help you?" he asked. The receptionist lingered behind him. "I hear the phones ringing, Miss Lind," the man said over his shoulder.

The young woman glanced back at Alberto and winked at him.

"I'm here to apply for the reporter position," Alberto said, removing his hat.

The man pinched off his little round glasses and stared at Alberto with bulging eyes. "But you're . . . why, you're Mexicano, aren't you?"

Alberto held out his damp right hand. "Albert Morales," he said, trying to pronounce his name the way Rosemary pronounced it. He waited for the man to notice his hand. "From the graduating class of '17, El Paso High School. I'm an American citizen."

The man wiped his hand on his vest and shook the tips of Alberto's fingers but did not bother to introduce himself.

"So, you can read and write English?"

"I was a member of the Sam Houston Debating Society in high school."

Why had he said that? A simple yes would have been enough. Alberto felt like a fool. He would have left already, but Rosemary's words were relentless: *You deserve a better job, Albert. You're an American citizen.* She hadn't been elected President of the Girls' Student Council just to marry a milkman.

"May I get an application, please?" Alberto said, his voice tightening at the back of his throat.

"Well, now," the man said, scratching the top of his ear with his glasses, "That's not up to me. I'm just the managing editor around here. Let me run it by the boss. What's your name again?"

"Albert Morales, Sir."

"Right. Moralees, you wait right here. I won't be long."

The man disappeared behind the glass door. Alberto unfolded his handkerchief again and wiped his whole face. His collar felt sticky from all the sweat. He was even sweating behind the ears. Miss Lind had not taken her eyes off him. He could smell his nerves stinking up his armpits.

"Can I get you a cool glass of water?" he heard Miss Lind's voice, but it sounded far away.

His mouth felt so dry. "I'm fine, thank you," he said.

But it was Rosemary banging around in his head. *You've got to stop thinking of yourself as a peon, Albert. You have talent. Remember what Mr. Fowler said. If you put your mind to it, you could be a journalist. Show 'em your stories. Especially the one you wrote about those Bath Riots. Mr. Fowler said that was your best piece.*

Alberto clasped the thick canvas of the rucksack hanging off his left arm. He had his stories in there, as well as his framed diploma.

Besides, Rosemary had reminded him, *the* Herald *stands up for people like you. You remember that article last week about how the mayor should clean up the barrios, how unfair it is to let people live in those conditions.*

Doesn't mean they want people like me writing their articles.

Well, you just tell 'em to practice what they preach, then! They want folks to be fair to Mexicans, let them set the example. Go on, Albert! You're a high school graduate. You're no ditchdigger. Daddy would buy that bungalow in Five Points for us if you got a real job. It has six rooms, Albert, a big sleeping porch, and a backyard with a lawn and a chicken house. The girls would love that.

Are we even allowed to live in Five Points, Rosemary?

We can live anywhere we want, especially if Daddy buys the place. I'm tired of living in this roach-infested icebox of an apartment.

That $22-a-month apartment was all Alberto could afford on his $10-a-week milkman wages. He had no idea she hated it so much.

I'm not like you, Rosemary. Look at me. You and the girls might pass, but I don't. They're not going to let us live in that neighborhood.

Stop jinxing us, Albert. Everything's gonna be just fine. You just have to get yourself a real job so Daddy knows we can afford the monthly payments.

It's $40 a month. That's almost double what we pay now.

And we'll have double the space, too. We have a third baby on the way, Albert. We need a separate bedroom for the kids.

I don't know, Rosemary, I don't like the idea of your dad being our landlord.

Can you stop being such a stubborn Mexican for once? You have a growing family to support. You need to get that job, Albert. We are not raising our girls in a tenement.

"Would you follow me, please?" Miss Lind was calling him from the doorway.

Alberto pocketed the handkerchief, and plopped the hat back on his head, brim askew. His knees bounced a little as he followed Miss Lind's blonde bobbed haircut into the clatter of typewriters and the bitter smell of old coffee that permeated the newsroom.

"All the way down the hall and to the left. You'll see Mr. Gaines."

Alberto felt his hand fidgeting with his hat again, and he took it off as he walked to where Miss Lind had pointed. The noise of the typewriters died down. He knew that every eye in the place was glued to the color of his skin. Alberto did not look around. *Tell 'em to practice what they preach*, he heard Rosemary's voice again, but he felt like a coyote sneaking through somebody's backyard.

"Here he is. Come on in, Moralees," said Gaines. "Say hello to Mr. Corbitt, editor-in-chief. Chief, this muchacho is an American citizen. He wants to be a reporter."

"Albert Morales," said Alberto, sticking his hand out.

Red-faced Mr. Corbitt was bald and had puffy bags under his beady blue eyes. He wore his shirt open at the collar, with no tie, and his nail-bitten fingers were stained with ink.

"Gaines tells me you're a bona fide high school graduate," said Corbitt in a thick Texas twang.

"From the graduating class of 1917, Sir," said Alberto, wringing his hat like a mop.

"Got your diploma with you, I assume?"

Alberto didn't know what to do with his hat. He stuffed it under his arm, placed the rucksack on his shoes to untie it and pulled out his El Paso High School diploma.

"My wife had it framed, Sir," Alberto said, handing it to Corbitt.

Corbitt scrutinized the diploma. "How do I know this is yours?" he said "Where's your birth certificate?"

"Birth certificate?" Alberto echoed. Why hadn't he thought of bringing that? "I don't have it with me, Sir, but I could catch a trolley and go get it right away. I'd be back in less than an hour.

If you want to see my writing, meanwhile, I do have these stories I wrote for my senior English class."

Alberto pulled out the brown envelope and offered it to Corbitt. Corbitt didn't take it.

"The teacher said that I . . ." Alberto swallowed the spit that was drying up in his mouth. ". . . that I had talent. That I could be a journalist someday."

Corbitt squinted at him as though trying to read the fine print on his face. "Did you serve your country?"

"My older brother got drafted, Sir. I was married already with a child on the way, so I'm the one that got to finish high school." He omitted the fact that his elderly parents had no one else to look after them.

The editor-in-chief didn't seem interested in his stories, so Alberto slipped the envelope back into his rucksack. Why didn't he have the guts to talk to them the way Rosemary would? He was the man of the family, but Rosemary was the one who had the guts. She knew that she didn't want to be called Mexican, ever. Even though her mother was Mexican, her father and her skin were white, and that's why she would have insisted that Corbitt read those stories. She would have read them herself, out loud, so that these white men could hear the talent that had written those words. Alberto didn't have Rosemary's advantages, and he didn't really want them, either. But Rosemary had her heart set on moving to a real house with a backyard for the girls, and Alberto had promised he would try.

"Sir, I wrote a piece about the young woman who started the Bath Riots at the Santa Fe bridge in 1917. Her name was—"

"Wait," Corbitt interrupted, snapping his fingers. "Didn't *The Times* cover that story?"

"It was quite the kerfuffle," said Gaines, chuckling. "All them crazy Mexican girls blocking the bridge and the streetcars for three days. Not even the Mexican army could make them budge."

Alberto felt his neck heating up again. "They weren't crazy, Sir. The women just didn't want to get fumigated to cross into El Paso. They were going to work. They didn't have lice."

"You're not being objective there, Moralees," said Gaines. "Fumigate's a harsh word. There was an epidemic of typhus going

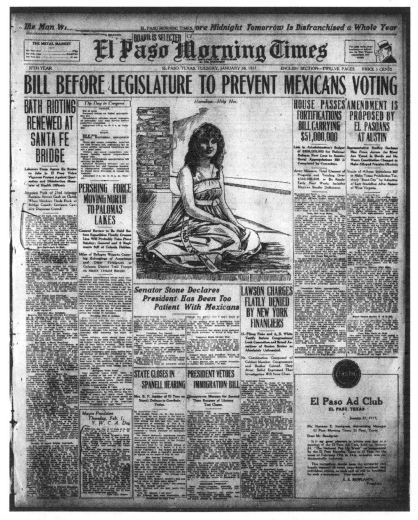

Figure 1. *El Paso Morning Times*, January 30, 1917. "Bill to Prevent Mexicans Voting" and "Bath Rioting Renewed at Santa Fe Bridge." Downloaded from www.thenation.com on 5/18/2022.

around, and most of it was coming in from Mexico. That's why the mayor ordered those disinfections. It wasn't just about the lice."

But Alberto knew the real story. The instigator of the protest, Carmelita Torres, worked with his mom cleaning the Kress Building. She was fed up with the kerosene baths that the Mexican workers were required to take before crossing the border, their clothes steamed in a chemical that burned their skin.

Corbitt's eyes were looking right through him. "Let's cut to the chase here, Moralees. Truth is, I hired someone for that reporter position just an hour ago, and even if I hadn't, I wouldn't be able to hire you, son." He returned Alberto's diploma. "Have you tried *El Fronterizo* over in Juárez? That paper just opened its doors last year. I'm sure you could put your talent to good use over there."

Alberto sighed. That was the problem with getting his hopes up, something Rosemary could never understand. "I don't write in Spanish, Sir," he said.

Corbitt and Gaines both frowned. Alberto put his hat back on, shouldered the rucksack and was about to leave. Gaines held up a hand to stop him.

"Not so fast, Moralees. We're not done here."

I am, thought Alberto, sick to his stomach that he had failed Rosemary's expectations.

"The reporter position may not be available," said Gaines. "But we do have something else. What are we calling it, Chief?"

"This was your idea," said Corbitt, hooking his thumbs in his sweaty armpits.

Alberto shook his head. No doubt they were going to offer him a custodian job. Inside, Rosemary was screaming: *I starched your shirt and cleaned your filthy bag so you could get hired as a janitor?*

"Moralees?"

Alberto blinked back his humiliation. "But I want to be a reporter, Sir."

"And I want to be President of the United States," said Corbitt. "But I'm not rightly qualified for that, am I? And you're not either, no matter what big ideas your English teacher put into your head. Mexicans just can't work office jobs. Not my rules."

"I'm not Mexican, Sir. I was born in El Paso. I'm an American citizen. Doesn't an American citizen have the right to apply to any job he wants?"

Corbitt narrowed his eyes at Gaines and drummed his fingers on the table. Alberto could tell they were communicating by some secret form of Morse code.

"So, the Chief and I were talking about how hard it is to get news out of the barrio," Gaines said, rolling up his shirtsleeves. "*The Herald* needs an inside man there, someone who can connect us to the folks, you know what I mean? Your people don't trust us, Moralees. They won't let us canvas. They slam the door in our reporters' faces. How are we supposed to report what happens over there if nobody, but the police or the coroner's office, gives us any information?"

"I'm not following you, Sir," said Alberto.

"How would you like to be our . . ." Gaines paused and thought about the job title. "Research specialist, that's it," he said, shaking his index finger at Alberto.

"I don't know what that is, Sir."

"Mr. Gaines here seems to think you could do some research for our reporters," said Corbitt. "In your barrio, especially. We need an inside man in Chihuahuita."

"My family never lived in Chihuahuita, Sir. Our home is in the Chamizal area."

"But you look like them and you speak their language," said Gaines, "which is a lot more than any of our guys."

"How much would a job like that pay, Sir?"

Corbitt nibbled on his thumb nail. "$15 dollars a week to start, and if you pan out and get us the information we need to run some good stories, we'll bump you up to $18 . . ."

"We'll throw in streetcar fare, too," added Gaines. "You'll be working in the field every day, but if you play your cards right, and you really do know how to write, you could be cranking out your own stories in a few years."

Alberto was thinking about that title: Research Specialist. Sounded like a fancy name for a spy. Or a *vendido*. That's what his father would call him, a *pinche vendido*, selling out his people for a house in Five Points.

Alberto's chest felt heavy, as if he'd been holding his breath all day. *They can crush your heart, Mi'jo, but don't let them break your huevos. It's the only advantage we have.* That was his father's favorite saying. Alberto exhaled slowly, so that his indignation wouldn't show.

"I can't support my wife and three kids on $15 a week, Sir. But I can start being your inside guy, your Research Specialist, right away. For $20 a week. That's a standard wage for high school graduates, isn't it?"

Corbitt was squinting at Gaines again. Whatever unsaid words were passing between them, Alberto could tell he had gotten the job. In his hand he was clutching his handkerchief again. He stared at the initials *AM*. *I AM*, he thought.

"Call Peters in here," Corbitt said.

Gaines stepped out of the office and yelled out, "Peters! Chief wants to see you!"

A minute later, a mustachioed young fellow in suspenders limped into the room, steeped in cigarette smoke.

"What's up?" he said. "I have a deadline." Peters had a pencil tucked behind one ear, a cigarette behind the other.

"Peters," said Corbitt, "meet Albert Moralees. He's going to be your research specialist."

Alberto felt a pinch in his chest.

"My what?" said Peters, eyeing Alberto from hair to socks.

"He's going to be your link to Chihuahuita," said Gaines. "Your inside man."

"Chaweeda ain't my beat, Chief," Peters said.

"It is now, Peters," said Corbitt. "We're giving you a column. *The Border Beat*. And Moralees here, he's going to get the news, and you're going to write it. Any complaints?"

"Hell no, Chief! A column? Hot tamalees! Hey, Moralees, your name rhymes with tamalees!"

The pinch had moved down to Alberto's groin.

"Is it just Chihuahuita we're going to report on, Sir, or the other barrios, too?"

"There's more than one barrio?" said Peters.

"Do you see how much we need this muchacho, Chief?" said Gaines.

"Show the man around, Peters," said Corbitt. "Then give him an assignment. Might as well break in that column pronto." The chief turned to Alberto. "When you bring in your birth certificate, we'll get your contract ready. $20 a week! You drive a hard bargain, son."

Corbitt shook Alberto's hand.

"Congratulations, Moralees!" Gaines said, slapping Alberto on the back. "Way to stick to your guns! Maybe you can use that Bath Riots piece you wrote for the inaugural story."

"That's old news, Sir," said Alberto.

"I disagree," said Gaines. "It's local color for *The Border Beat*."

"But that protest happened four years ago," said Alberto.

"Let me ask you something, Moralees," Corbitt interjected. "Are they still doing those disinfections at the bridge?"

Alberto clenched his jaws and nodded.

"Then it's not old news, is it?" Corbitt said. "I want you to go on down there and talk to some folks, give us a real inside scoop on what's taking place."

"Maybe we could send a photographer down there with him," said Gaines.

"Good idea," said Corbitt. "Now, if you all don't mind, I have a paper to run."

Alberto did not thank anybody as he followed Peters out of Corbitt's office.

"This here's *my* desk," said Peters. "My typewriter. My chair. My ashtray. My phone. My pencils. You're gonna work on the street. Now, where's that story you're supposed to give me?"

Alberto dug the Carmelita Torres story out of his rucksack and gave it to Peters.

"This is messy as hell. Didn't you learn how to type?"

"That class was for girls only," said Alberto.

Peters arched an eyebrow. "From now on, you got to submit your notes in a Reporter's Notebook. Go get yourself a notebook from Honey Pie over there," Peters continued. He jerked his thumb in the direction of Miss Lind, who was filing her nails at the front counter.

"How'd it go?" the receptionist asked, stowing the nail file in her purse.

"I need a notebook," Alberto said.

"No kidding?" she said, genuinely surprised.

"No kidding," Alberto said.

"Good for you. What's your name again?"

"Alberto Morales, at your service."

"I'm Shirley. Receptionist, typist and everybody's Girl Friday."

She opened a drawer of the filing cabinet behind the counter, took a long, thin notebook from a stack and handed it to Alberto. On the cover, it said Reporter's Notebook.

Peters sauntered over and dropped Alberto's story on Miss Lind's typewriter. "Be a doll, and type this up. I need it by 4 p. m., sharp."

"This ain't your writing," Miss Lind said. "I can read it for a change."

"Did I ask you for your opinion on my handwriting" asked Peters.

Miss Lind rolled her eyes. "Whose story is this gonna be?" she asked. "Yours or his?"

"For your information, Mr. Corbitt just gave me a new column," said Peters. "That's the inaugural story right there. Call it The Border Beat: a Column by Franklin Peters."

They're gonna plagiarize my best piece, Rosemary. I hope you're happy. Alberto realized he had made a mistake in sharing his work with them.

Peters approached Alberto on the other side of the receptionist's counter, so close his tobacco breath hung like a spiderweb between the man's mouth and Alberto's neck. "Now, go out and get me some news," said Peters. "But don't be giving me any opinions, Moralees. All I want from you is facts. Nothing but facts. Keep your bean-brained opinions to yourself. Flunkies don't give opinions, do they, Miss Lind?"

No *señor*, thought Alberto, gripping his hat in his fist. He was no ditchdigger. A ditchdigger would've already punched this *cabrón*'s teeth out of his mouth.

But he could hear Rosemary already. *I knew you could do it, Albert.* She would wrap her arms around his neck, press against him so tight he could feel the peaks on her brassiere, and kiss him long and slow like she used to under the bleachers of El Paso High.

No doubt, she would want to go down to the drugstore right away to telephone her father and give him the good news.

Albert got a real job, Daddy. He's training to be a reporter for the El Paso Herald. *He's getting twice the salary he makes now, and they even gave him a Reporter's Notebook.*

3
TEN FRONTERIZA MEDITATIONS ON LA LLORONA

1.

For my "pure-bred" middle-class-adjacent, light-skinned Mexican family, the legend of La Llorona was *puro cuento*, or just a tall tale told to children to keep us from staying out past dark, or else the ghostly lady wandering the streets of our barrio at night, calling out for her lost children, would steal us away. We heard stories of La Llorona sightings from my cousins in Juárez; reports of a ghostly woman in white with long black hair seen wandering by the train tracks or near the ASARCO smoke-stacks; hovering by the lake in Ascarate Park or bending over a grave in Concordia Cemetery, where the ghosts of dead children play among the headstones. Margarita, my grandparents' live-in housekeeper, told me she saw La Llorona every time she returned from visiting her family in Juárez, and swore that, from her mother's neighborhood near El Malecón, the long dark highway that runs parallel to the river, she could hear La Llorona's cry every night.

"When I was little like you," she told me, pointing to my grandmother's Guardian Angel candle, "I thought the Guardian Angel was La Llorona protecting people from *la* Migra." That's what I think of even now, whenever I look at the image of the Guardian Angel protecting those two children as they walk over a broken bridge: That's La Llorona.

2.

I was born in the occupied territory north of the Rio Grande, land of the betrayer and the betrayed. My history begins in a maternity clinic in downtown El Paso where my 18-year-old mother gave birth to me, her first of the three children she had with my father. Two years later, she gave birth to my little brother, and one year after that, my little sister. By the time I was five years old, two old conflicts came to an end: my parents got divorced, and the Rio Grande changed its course for the last time.

I had been living with my grandparents since birth, practically, because my mom worked long shifts as the cashier of a furniture store in downtown El Paso and was too exhausted to tend to her kid, her house and her husband during the week. But on Saturdays, my dad would bring her to my grandmother's house to do their laundry, while he sat around drinking with his brothers, engaging in declamation contests to see who could recite the full text of Sor Juana's "Hombres necios." My brother and I played with our cousins in the backyard, and the rest of the family crooned over the green-eyed little doll that was my baby sister. After lunch, my mother and the housekeeper washed and dried all the dishes, then she went outside to collect her clean laundry. After the last piece of stiff, sun-dried clothing had been taken down from the clothesline and folded into her basket, my mother tells me, they bundled me up with my brother and sister and took me back to Juárez with them to spend the night; but I don't remember any of that. Did I have my own bed, or did I share sleeping space with my parents or my siblings? I don't remember anything about that house, but I do remember that on Sundays, after a breakfast of beans and quesadillas at my great grandparents' house, my brother and I played with another set of cousins until late into the afternoon. We threw water balloons, played *a la roña* and *a las escondidas*, tag and hide-and-seek, in the big patio of the *solar* that connected the homes of three generations of my mother's family: my great-grandmothers' house, my mom's house and the house of Abuelita's youngest sister who ran a flamenco dance school to support herself and her four kids. I always found it strange that my mother called my great-grandmother Mamá, and her own mom by her first name. Later I learned that my mother had been raised by her grandmother, just as I was being raised by mine.

I remember how my great-grandmother stirred canned milk into her Nescafé while my mom ironed my father's clothes. I have a clear memory of my great-grandfather chasing us around with a scary mask over his face that he'd cut out of a paper bag, and the kids screeching, *¡Córrele, o te agarra El Paquetudo!* Run, or El Paquetudo is gonna get you! To me El Paquetudo was much scarier than La Llorona because I knew that he was real, and he could pop out of hiding when we least expected it. There was always so much going on over there in Juárez, in the *solar* where my mom lived, and sometimes, people would fight and yell late into the night, and other times there would be loud laughing and cookouts for no reason.

On Sunday nights, my grandparents from El Paso would drive across the bridge to pick me up and take me back home with them for the rest of the week. The only thing missing from those early memories is my father. The hardest thing to get used to after the divorce was not seeing my mom every weekend. As part of the divorce orders, my father (or, really, his parents) was given custody of me, and my brother and sister went to my mother. She was allowed to visit me only three times a year, on my birthday, Mother's Day and Christmas, and only for an hour, and only sitting with her in her parked car rather than inside the house with a glass of *limonada*. Because of some deep embarrassment she had caused my father that proved she was a "bad wife" and a "bad mother," my father's parents never wanted to see her again, so she was not allowed to park in front of their house during our visit. My brother was welcome to stay with us whenever he wanted, and for the time he was there, I had a little buddy to play Hot Wheels with me, and marbles and spaceships and Tarzan. But he was deeply attached to our mother and after a few months, he missed her so much he cried all the time, and we had to take him back to Juárez again to live with her and the ugly man who had taken my father's place.

3.

As a child, I never understood how my mother could like that ugly man more than my beautiful father with his cleft chin and his three-piece suits; but then, I didn't know anything about alcoholism, serial infidelity and narcissism. Apparently, the ugly man possessed all the qualities my beautiful father lacked: he worked for a living, driving a city bus; he didn't have other women on the side; he didn't drink alcohol; and with the money he gave her to pay the bills and buy the groceries, my mother managed to save enough to give the down payment on their first house in El Paso. Her life wasn't perfect, though. For years, the ugly man beat and terrorized my brother so much that sometimes my mother would drive him across the border and leave him at my grandparents' chain-link fence with two paper bags full of his clothes and toys. She knew that there he would heal from his wounds: the belt-marks, the burn marks from where he'd been pushed up against a wall heater, the bruises. I remember standing at the living room window watching his skinny body and disheveled blond hair trudge up the walkway, holding on to his paper bags, and I felt the scariest feeling bubbling up inside me: hatred. Pure, total and unforgiving hatred for that awful man who inflicted such damage on my little brother.

I wished him dead. Closing my eyes, I summoned the image of my Ouija board, imagined my hand hovering over the planchette and flying over the letters that spelled his name. I HATE HIM. I WANT HIM TO DIE. GOODBYE. Truth is, I wanted to kill him myself. And the more I hated him, the more my anger poisoned my relationship with my mother. The more I resented her for having chosen this cruel and horrible man, the more my grandparents called her a bad mother who preferred the company of this inhuman being to that of her three children together under her husband's roof. Years later, as a newly married adult, I asked my mother why she split up the family, told her how hard it had been for me to grow up as a single child in El Paso while my brother and sister were growing up in Juárez with her and the rest of her family. She was a smoker, then, and as we sat across her kitchen table together, she told me the truth of her decision, smoking one cigarette after another. She knew she wanted more for herself and her kids than the torment of a cuckolded and unstable economic life with my father, but she had no idea what fate awaited her, or her children, with her new husband. At the time of the divorce, she agreed to let me stay with my paternal grandparents, Pa'Carlos and Mima, who had raised me from a baby anyway, and my little sister could go with her mother, Abuelita T, to be raised in safety. Her son, she figured, as a growing *hombrecito* would probably be okay staying with her and her second husband. Although my sister and I will always be grateful to her for her decision to place us with our grandparents, our little man didn't fare so well.

I think it was when my brother started showing up at my grandparents' doorstep with signs of that man's abuse that La Llorona began haunting me in my dreams. Late at night, lying on the thin mattress of my fold-up cot, I would listen for La Llorona's voice, her lonely cry summoning the souls of the children she had drowned and that she would spend eternity trying to find. La Llorona was my mother, and I her abandoned daughter living with relatives north of the river, and my brother, her battered son cowering at her side, and my baby sister, whom I hardly knew, had her name changed without my parents' permission.

"I never asked your grandmother to adopt your sister," my mother said. "And neither did your father." But because Abuelita T and her husband had raised my sister from the time she was nine months old, they arbitrarily gave her their last name on all her school documents, thereby detaching her from the Gaspar de Alba lineage. She was legally adopted by them at thirteen, not only erasing our father's last name from her life, but also, removing her as our sibling. Instead of my mother's daughter, she became my mother's sister; instead of our little sister, she became our aunt (that's how she's listed in our family tree on Ancestry.com). On the El Paso side, I was raised as Pa'Carlos and Mima's youngest child, displacing their youngest daughter, who became my sister instead of my aunt. And that's a whole other resentment tale.

4.

For a hundred years after the signing of the Treaty of Guadalupe-Hidalgo, the Rio Grande was shifty. The international boundary line between Mexico and the United States kept changing each time the river changed its course. This caused all sorts of problems between the two nations, none of which I was even aware of, until finally, in 1963, when the Rio Grande shifted its course for the last time, a new agreement was signed called the Chamizal Treaty, which returned 630 acres of El Paso, Texas back to Mexico. The border had to be redrawn, new bridges and inspection stations had to be constructed, and all the area known as El Chamizal had to be returned to Mexico, free of charge, including homes and buildings and businesses. The clinic where I was born stood on that repatriated land and was now located in Mexico. If my place of birth was in Mexico, I wondered, would I still be an American citizen?

By then, I was six years old, and had just started first grade. I had bigger problems to worry about because I didn't speak English yet. I understood it well enough, thanks to watching my favorite TV shows—*Lassie, Leave It To Beaver, Star Trek* and *Gilligan's Island*—as well as reruns of *The Honeymooners* with my grandfather, but I could not say the Pledge of Allegiance in the classroom, or sing from the hymnbook in the school church, and no amount of threats to my eternal soul by the Mother Superior could make me sing the National Anthem at school assemblies.

I remember my father's younger sister, my aunt Carmen, only 12 years older than me, teaching me my first word in English. We were watching one of those old romantic movies she loved to watch on Saturday afternoons, and I noticed people kept calling each other Honey.

"What does that word *honey* mean?" I asked in Spanish.

"That's what you call somebody really special that you love with all your heart," she said, her eyes fixed on the TV.

"Then you're my *honey*," I said.

She put her arm around me and squeezed me against her rib. "And you're mine," she said, kissing me on the forehead.

From then on, I and all my cousins from the El Paso side called her Honey (RIP).

I have absolutely no memory of how long it took for me to learn to read, write and speak in English, or of when I started to feel like I really belonged in the classroom. How I went from that tongue-tied little kid to the spelling bee champion of the school is one of those dark mysteries that perhaps only La Llorona can explain. I wasn't allowed to speak English at home, though, unless I was translating for my grandmother. And the nuns punished or fined us if we were caught speaking Spanish at school unless we were in Spanish class. I grew up with a forked tongue and a severe case of cultural schizophrenia, the split in the psyche that happens to someone who grows up in the borderlands between nations, languages and cultures.

5.

Figure 2. US President Lyndon B. Johnson and Mexican President Adolfo
López Mateos at the unveiling of the Chamizal National Monument, 1964.
Downloaded on May 8, 2022 from The National Park Service/US Department of the Interior website, https://www.nps.gov/nr/travel/american_
latino_heritage/chamizal_national_memorial.html.

The shifting of the Rio Grande displaced more than 5,000 people from their homes and livelihoods. President Lyndon B. Johnson came to El Paso to shake hands with the Mexican President in
the football stadium at Bowie High School. With that handshake,
the United States agreed to transfer 630 acres from Texas back to
Mexico according to the terms of the Chamizal Treaty of 1964.[1]
The story about the event in the *El Paso Times* was full of pictures of the two presidents and the shiny monument at which they
shook hands, behind them a map of the new borderline cutting
across Cordova Island. I really didn't understand what all the hype
was about or what this transfer of lands meant.

"What does El Chamizal mean?" I asked one morning at breakfast.

"It's the only piece of the stolen land ever restored to Mexico," my grandfather said, as if I had any idea what he meant by the stolen land.

Whatever it was, we weren't learning about in school. The nuns of Loretto were teaching us about not forgetting the Alamo.

"Whoever that land belongs to, I just hope they clean up the stench," Mima, my ever-practical grandmother, said. That was where the stockyards and the sewage plant were located, and in the hot afternoons, the septic reek of cow, pig and human manure wafted through our barrio, gagging even the dogs.

The brother-in-law of my favorite uncle who liked to help me with my English explained to me with a simple drawing of a squiggly line that because the river had moved and shifted the location of the clinic that was my birthplace, I was a Mexican now. He was wrong about that, but I didn't know that then. For some reason, changing nationalities made me profoundly happy. The next time I went with my grandparents to the Juárez *mercado*, I was so looking forward to saying "Mexican" instead of "American" to the Border Patrol agent waving cars with Texas plates into El Paso.

"*No seas chistosa, Alicia,*" Mima chided. But I wasn't trying to be funny.

"Pa'Carlos," I said, tugging on my grandfather's earlobe, "*¿no que nací en México?* Wasn't I born in Mexico?"

My grandfather shrugged. "Who knows?" he said, grinning into the rearview mirror. "*¡Pregúntale al presidente!*" Why would the president know, I wondered? Pa'Carlos laughed so much at his own joke, he started coughing and dropped his cigarette on the front seat and burned a hole in the red leather of his station wagon.

My grandmother turned to glare at me with her sharp green eyes. "Don't you dare say you're anything but American," she scolded me, pinching my ear for good measure. "We don't have any papers for you! Do you want us to leave you here at the bridge like one of those orphans?"

Maybe I was like the avocados she'd bought at the *mercado*, hiding the Mexican seed inside them, that she always smuggled across the bridge in her purse.

6.

In Juárez, La Llorona claimed El Chamizal as the territory of the dispossessed. It was on this repatriated land full of thickets of saltbush and mesquite that the Mexicans built El Parque Chamizal, a big federal public park, popular with families, lovers, athletes and stray dogs. The park is so huge it sports an Olympic stadium, a lake, pony rides with real-live ponies, a performance space where famous people of the caliber of Vicente Fernández, Lucha Villa and Juan Gabriel gave public concerts, fairgrounds for the annual Expo Feria of the goods, products and services of Ciudad Juárez and the state of Chihuahua. On the El Paso side, the gringos also built a park, the Chamizal National Memorial, with a museum and a cultural center and an entrance fee.

The Chamizal Treaty straightened out the meandering borderline and channeled the Rio Grande between cement embankments and chain-link fencing known as the Tortilla Curtain. On the El Paso side of the fence, the sprawling international *puente libre*, or free bridge, officially known as Bridge of the Americas between the United States and Mexico, was constructed over Córdova Island, a no-man's land just above El Chamizal populated by *maleantes, borrachos y raboverdes*, according to my grandmother. Bad men, drunks and perverts. And it was beneath that bridge in the badlands between the two nations, also known as the Barrio del Diablo, that La Llorona was said to live. The Clardy Fox barrio where I grew up was north of El Chamizal, just on the other side of what is now the Border Highway, and on windy days, especially during Lent, tumbleweeds hurtled down the street like hollow souls escaping from La Llorona.

7.

Whether she was a legend or a tall tale, a ghost or an angel, La Llorona haunted my childhood. I was into gothic lore long before Goth became an attitude and a fashion statement in this country. On Sunday afternoons when all my uncles came over with their families, I liked tuning into the televised bullfights on the Mexican channel instead of the Speedy González cartoons my cousins kept whining for me to let them watch. As the oldest of the cousins, and the only one who got to live with our grandparents, I called the shots. I decided not only what we watched on TV, but whether we played *a la familia*, hide-and-seek or kick-the-can. I was also very much into the occult: seances, the Ouija board, ghost stories. Nothing was more fun or fascinating to me than sitting around with my cousins telling stories about La Llorona. She could be anything and anywhere: a beautiful young woman in a long white dress, a door-to-door tamale-vendor or the old beggar woman that I often saw asking for coins on the bridge. According to our elders, she was the evil spirit looking for rebellious children to kidnap and drown in the river. If we never wanted to see the skeletal face of La Llorona or feel her long sharp nails digging into our backs as we ran home after dark, we'd better do as we were told and come home before the sun set.

But I loved being outside in the dark. I was a child of the night, a lover of vampires and werewolves and witches like the ones that populated my favorite TV show, *Dark Shadows*. Ghosts didn't scare me. Neither did the Ouija board, or the seances I played at with the neighbor kids and little brother (when he was around). At 12, I remember walking into a place called The Emporium, across the street from the public library downtown. I wandered under all the crystals hanging in that store, all the powders and potions in little glass vials, as though I had just stepped into Dr. Julia Hoffman's secret laboratory on *Dark Shadows*, perusing the used books on divination, astrology and witchcraft crammed into the only bookshelf in the store. They sold voodoo kits with black and red candles, all kinds of incense in sticks and cones, mysterious dark soap and bottles of magic oil. The whole store smelled like magic. In a glass case by the register, there were several decks of Tarot cards on display, along with big hunks of amethyst and turquoise and silver pentagrams hanging from silver chains. Why had nobody told me there could be stores like this? With my allowance money, I bought a pair of black votive candles, and my brother swears (although I think he's making it up) that I liked to take those candles into the closet, light them up and conduct seances all by myself, with the help of the Ouija board.

"*Esta cabrona* has always been a witch!" my brother told my mother, once. "She's never been afraid of anything, not even the Devil!"

But he was wrong. It was the priests and the nuns at my Catholic elementary school who terrified me. The priests with their foamy spit and brimstone lectures and the nuns with their rulers and paddles, their accusatory eyes. Although I didn't admit it, my grandmother's arthritic hand smacking me on the mouth for talking back was pretty scary. Her angry face was way more frightening to me than La Llorona; at least I could run away from La Llorona and not get in trouble; but I was not allowed to run from my grandmother when she was trying to "correct" this rude, ungrateful granddaughter, whom she had taken in and who paid her back with such disobedience.

Despite our constant friction, I loved Mima, or Ma, as I started calling her after my grandfather died. I loved her food, especially her rice and beans, which I could eat day and night. I loved helping her trace patterns for the dresses and culottes she sewed for me, translating for her from the Sears & Roebuck catalog from which she ordered my school uniforms. I knew she was always in pain because the arthritis was twisting up her fingers and her hunching back made her shorter as I got taller. I remember rubbing marijuana-steeped alcohol all over her spine at night, and in the afternoons, after school, after we'd eaten and I'd finished my homework, she would set her big pot of paraffin on the stove, melt it down and bring it to the table so that I could help her slip her hands into the hot wax over and over, making thick white waxy gloves that I would wrap up in a kitchen towel for her so that she could sit quietly and relax while the hot gloves worked their magic on her aching joints and digits.

The wax treatment was our ritual, our time to bond. Tell me about Pedro Infante, I would goad her, and she was always happy to tell the story of being serenaded by the young crooner back in the days when they lived in Sinaloa. She was about 19 or 20 years old at the time, and already had three of her eight children, including my dad. Pedro Infante was just getting his career started and on late nights of behaving badly, my grandfather would pay his buddy Pedro to offer *una serenata* to my grandmother. Orphaned by her mother, raised by a strict maternal aunt, Mima only got as far as the second grade, and her penmanship showed it. At 14, she was married off to my grandfather, who was twice her senior, and started having babies at 15.

I loved my grandmother's stories. She would get so engrossed in them, the sweat would bead up on her forehead and run down to the tip of her nose, as the heat of the wax treatment seeped into her hands. In the den, the television droned the nightly news with Walter Cronkite. Somewhere on the other side of the bridge, my mother was living her own life without me.

8.

La Llorona is the enigmatic figure that signifies my past, my umbilical connection to my mother and my culture. She has haunted my creative work since my very first publication in 1972, as an eighth grader whose badly written, multi-syllabic one-paragraph analogy about my grandfather's passing as a monstrous predator called "Death" was published in *New America Speaks*, a volume of writings by high school students published by the American Studies Program at the University of New Mexico. Little did I know that this 1972 publication portended the dissertation I would write 22 years later for my PhD in American Studies from the University of New Mexico and the novel I would publish 33 years later on the murdered young women of Juárez. I wrote a research paper on La Llorona in the one and only Chicano Literature course offered in the English Department at the University of Texas at El Paso (*la* UTEP to us border folks), in which I learned that my family had lied to me when they insisted that Mexicans were different from Chicanos. How could we be so different when the ghostly weeping lady that Mima was always rousing to scare us kids into obedience was the same one that these Chicanos were writing about in their poems and stories? It did not surprise me that La Llorona evolved into the controlling image of my writing, as we see throughout my first book of poetry, *Beggar on the Córdoba Bridge* (1989).

She is the star of the show in my second poetry collection, *La Llorona on the Longfellow Bridge* (2003), structured around the journeys I have taken 1985-2001; from my weekly visits to the Black Angel Cemetery in Iowa City, where I had moved to begin my doctoral studies until I dropped out nine months later; to Boston, where I had escaped academia to live the writer's life; to Albuquerque, where I completed the PhD and broke a good woman's heart when I fell in love with another; to Los Angeles, where I started my 30-year sojourn as a professor of Chicanx Studies at UCLA; to the Land of the Dead, where my Honey's ovarian cancer took her, where my father was waiting for her, where my half-brother ended up after a short life of crime and diabetes, his decomposed body identified only by the tattoos on his arms, one of them spelling my mother's name. From Oaxaca to Salem, Massachusetts, death is a spectacle—a witch museum or a cemetery decorated in *cempazuchitl* and *papel picado*—a daily ritual that, like the wind at Lent on the El Paso/Juárez border, "is more alive / than the people's memory."[2]

In Boston, on my daily walks through the Public Garden and my T-rides on the Red Line to my tarot classes in Cambridge, I could hear La Llorona moaning in the maple trees or in the shrill screech of metal wheels on the train tracks or in the crackling icy waters of the Charles River. In fact, sightings of La Llorona extend from coast to coast, from the Golden Gate to the Longfellow Bridge. In "Eclipse" she's spotted in New York City on 9/11, right after the collapse of the Twin Towers.

Can you see her?
There at Ground Zero:
that is not Liberty
walking among the dead,
wearing a hard hat
and a gas mask
black hair dragging in the ashes
of all those nameless Mexicans.
That woman wailing at the sooty sky
Is La Llorona. (*Longfellow Bridge*, 110)

La Llorona lives wherever Mexicans live, not just on the border or in the Southwest, but also in Alaska or Australia, Nova Scotia or New York. But now, hers is a more mundane existence, no longer as mythological as it used to be. In "Kyrie Eleison for La Llorona," I offer a Mass for this legendary figure, this "wicked mother" who for generations has borne the blame "for everybody's sins," and yet she is "still not canonized, Devil's martyr." The Mass does not mean La Llorona has died or that she's stopped "pulling stray kids and lovers/to her path," it's just a way of honoring "all her years/in our genealogy." Although her history goes back to before the Spanish Conquest, "haunting the cause-ways/of our island-hearts," her memory is tainted with destruc-tion like a "mushroom cloud hovering/over Mount Cristo Rey," and "what's left of [her] voice" is only heard now in the furtive passing of late-night trains through the desert or in the muffled sobs of beaten transwomen outside the gay bar. Maybe La Llorona has materialized somehow, after five centuries of search-ing in vain for the souls of her children; maybe she's left purga-tory and come back to an earthly existence where she needs a job. No longer does she traffic in mysteries and secrets. She's "traded [her] midnight cry for the graveyard/shift and a paycheck at the maquila." Once, she may have been the "Virgin of the de-ported" and "Mother of the dispossessed," but today her memory dissipates in the smoke of burning chrysanthemums. (*Longfel-low Bridge*, 106, 108).

And occasionally, after too many tequilas, we can still hear her eerie cry in the wild shrieks of mariachi songs at the Kentucky Club. Far away, in a Valentine's Day "Encuentro" at Harry's Bar in Los Angeles, a lonely academic named Butch has been jilted by her date, and she sits at the bar knocking back shots of tequila and scotch after a round of martinis, wallowing in the memory of a time when she had unknowingly picked up a transwoman named Vanessa, who, after a few drinks and some torrid kissing, refused to go to bed with her. The bartender named Walt, who's "big on contradictions," is worried about Butch. She's a regular, after all. He wants to clean up the mess of empty glasses on the bar in front of Butch, but she doesn't want "to lose count of how much [she] hates [herself]." She's on such a pity-pot bender, bemoaning her luck with women who either fail to show up or refuse to follow through, that she doesn't notice the strange and beautiful woman who has just taken the seat next to her. Walt sets a house drink in front of her, a lovely Valentine-themed martini of Campari and gin, that she lifts to toast with Butch.

"Do I know you?" Butch asked.
"You must," said the woman, "you've been on my
track for years."
(*Longfellow Bridge*, 115)

9.

La Llorona troubled me incessantly when I started my research on the murdered girls and women of Ciudad Juárez. In
1999, I landed a prestigious endowed chair position in the English Department at the University of Texas at El Paso. It was a
temporary gig, lasting only the Fall semester, but it proved to be
a pivotal moment in my academic and writer's life, for this is
when I really learned the lurid history of what would in a few
years become an epidemic of kidnapped, raped, tortured and vi-
ciously murdered young women that we now know as the Juárez
femicides or *feminicidios*—the killing of women for being
women, only in this case, it was the killing of poor, young "*indi-
tas del sur*" (one of the epithets given to the femicide victims by
the newspapers) overpopulating the border.

My mystery novel on the femicides, *Desert Blood: The
Juárez Murders* (2005), is set in the summer of 1998, at that moment when the American public has not yet started taking an interest in the kidnappings and killings of young women in Juárez,
nor are the authorities or the news media in El Paso alarmed yet
by the escalating numbers of dead female bodies across the river,
even though some of them are found to be American citizens.
Each crime is instructive, each crime scene is littered with tainted
or unfound evidence, each death is a portent of the destruction
and subjugation of the poor brown female body whose only crime
is being another poor brown female body on the doorstep of the
Promised Land.

Who was killing these women, but more importantly, why
were they being killed in such vicious ways? Rape and torture

were common factors among the victims, as was their demographic: young, poor, dark-skinned and dark-haired, indigenous-looking women, many of them migrants to the border looking for work in one of the city's hundreds of maquiladoras, while others were simply schoolgirls, little girls, good girls gone bad in the social discourse of Church and State. Why was there so much apathy on both sides of the border regarding these gendered deaths? How could I write a mystery novel about this unsolved, and apparently unstoppable, crime spree? Here were the most disenfranchised members of society, the most marginal of the marginalized. What power did these girls and women have, I kept asking myself, that made them the target of such misogynistic violence? How did they threaten the perpetrators or the institutional forces that hired and protected these perps? What was it about these female bodies that the killers, their employers and the border population in general hated so intensely? I couldn't figure it out.

Trying to connect the dots, I would read and reread the growing list of names, the glib descriptions of the heinous acts perpetrated against them. I took copious notes on the bodies and the modus operandi of their demise. I researched the first suspects, the task forces instituted by the local and state governments to supposedly address these crimes, the working conditions at the factories at which many of the victims worked for slave wages. I rode around with an El Paso detective and attended an autopsy. I interviewed activists north and south of the border and combed through the archives of those who were kind enough to share their own research with me. And then I saw it, so obvious it was easy to look right through it. The sheer brutality acted upon the victims' bodies, I realized, was a clue. So was the obsessive control and surveillance of their reproductive systems at the maquiladoras where many of them worked, the birth control shots or implants they were required to submit to if they hoped to keep their high-quota, high-stress jobs.

As far as I could tell, and this is the message of my novel, the only power these women relegated to the margins of our concern possess is their ability to give birth, to bring more brown children into the world. It's their fertility that is the target of these crimes, I realized! Pregnancy is inconvenient to the maquiladoras' productivity and profit margins. A reproductive body is not productive, does not produce its quota and must get paid just the same, according to Mexican labor laws. And there's always the chance—no, the high likelihood—that the pregnant body will find a way to deliver her child across the border and bring one more anchor baby into the ever-browning demographic of the United States.

Female fertility, or rather, the fertility of all those young, poor, brown women and girls who daily arrive from their towns and villages in the interior of Mexico or Central America seeking employment in the maquiladora industry is the most negative side effect of NAFTA that nobody, except perhaps La Llorona, predicted. Just as nobody told the young women they would be coming to a heavily industrialized urban border riddled with devastating social problems: poverty, overcrowding, violence, drug cartel wars, environmental hazards, femicides. Nobody told them this *frontera* is not built to sustain all those migrant workers who are trolling the industrial parks in search of a job or seeking services at the IMSS, the Mexican Social Security Institute, which is the socialized public health care system that Mexico provides for its working people. If they have no friends or family to welcome them or give them a place to live, many of these migrants must find shelter in the *colonias*—the unincorporated shantytowns—located on the outskirts of the city in all directions, where they have no access to basic city services: gas, electricity, running water, a sewage system or trash collection.

These *colonias* are usually located miles away from the industrial parks where they work, in pitch-black patches of scrub brush and desert that are not accessible by public roads or paved streets. Buses are contracted out by the maquiladoras to transport the workers to and from their jobs, but they only go as far as the pavement goes. No screening of drivers takes place; they could be and often are drug addicts, sex offenders or ex-convicts. The job goes to the lowest bidder. The terrible peril that looms over these young, brown, laboring bodies 24/7 as soon as they set foot in Ciudad Juárez is as unfathomable as *el laberinto del silencio*, the labyrinth of silence that awaits their bones. Is it any wonder that we have so many dead women on that border? Need we ask why La Llorona must work overtime to gather their souls together and take them with her to the solace of the river?

The bodies of the first victims of this genocidal crime wave cropped up in 1993, and still, over thirty years later, the killing of women continues, the impunity for the perpetrators is practically gospel, and no amount of journalistic reports, movies, plays, novels, academic studies, conferences, television exposés, art exhibitions, photos and songs about the *feminicidios*, nor the dedicated attention of federal and judicial task forces in Mexico, non-governmental organizations from all over the world, the United Nations, Amnesty International, the World Court is enough to stop these vicious murders of women and girls on the US-Mexico border. This is the injustice that La Llorona's indignant cry is meant to disrupt, the shrill song of dissent that breaks the silence of the victims, the angry lament of hundreds and thousands of brown, female bodies killed in their prime. Or maybe, it's the collective howl of the mothers of the victims who dread that they will never see their daughters again, who know from the condition of the remains (if they're lucky enough to get them back) or from the shocking pictures they see on television or in the sensationalized periodicals like *Alarma* that their child died in agony.

¡Ay, mi hija! ¿Dónde estará mi hija? ¿Qué le habrán hecho a mi hija?

Figure 3. *La Llorona Desperately Seeking Coyolxauhqui* by Alma Lopez, 2003. Used by permission of the artist.

10.

Alma Lopez's serigraph *La Llorona Desperately Seeking Coyolxauhqui* (2003) offers one possible answer for the mothers and the daughters of Juárez. Against a patterned background that reminds us of the Virgin of Guadalupe's robe, the image depicts one of the *feminicidio* victims who has been Coyolxauhquied, in other words, cut up into pieces by the killers, the media and the social discourse that blames them for their own deaths. The roses signify her innocence, the freshness of her life cut short. She seems to wear a veil over her face, but it's more of an ephemeral mask over her mouth in the shape of a necklace that alludes to Coatlicue, the Mother of the Gods and Goddess of Life and Death. The mask positioned over her mouth represents the silence that has prevented social empathy for the victims and waylaid justice, but also the way in which women are conditioned to keep quiet, to not tell anyone if they've been raped or sexually accosted. Except for the very few that escaped their predators, the femicide victims could not tell anyone what happened to them, but their bodies cried out silently, nonetheless.

And the mothers, especially the ones who have politicized themselves into raising public consciousness about their daughter's murders, speak truth to power. They denounce the perpetrators and the Mexican government for its apathy, misogyny and callous dismissals of their losses and their activism. For the mayor of Juárez, the governor of the state of Chihuahua and the president of the Mexican Republic, all the mothers' protests and manifestations, all their travels outside of Mexico to attend conferences and present their *testimonios* and claims of collusion and corruption, their critiques of the investigations, their demands for justice—all of these are actions that betray the nation and give Juárez a bad name, which negatively impact the two most important industries in Mexico: tourism and the maquiladora system.

While the mothers assemble and the government dissembles, more and more daughters get taken, raped, violently murdered, and cast into shallow graves, empty lots, landfills, vats of acid or black waters. While the authorities search in vain for their bodies, or for the clues that could help them identify the criminals, it is La Llorona who finds their souls, who opens her arms to embrace another warrior daughter to her ghostly bosom. La Llorona is her Guardian Angel walking *una hija más de la frontera* across the broken bridge to the land of the dead.

La Llorona is one of the primordial "bad women" of my collective history and culture, dating all the way back to pre-Columbian times. Like Sor Juana, La Malinche and Coyolxauhqui— all persecuted in their lifetimes for daring to rebel against the patriarchal social order enforced by Religion, Tradition and the Laws of the Family—La Llorona has been framed. Not only has she been accused of adultery and the unforgivable crime of drowning her own children, but also, she's been blamed for causing her own death because of her "bad woman" ways, that is, her disloyalty, her dis-obedience and her dis-ease with the status quo. She could be the anguished lonely soul or "Ánima Sola" who weeps and wastes away in the Purgatory of a perpetual pariah existence trying to atone for all her sins; or, she could be the ancient Mexica goddess of death, Cihuacuatl, the sixth omen that warned the Aztecs about the arrival of the invaders who would bring an end to their world, crying out in warning once again: "Beware the end of our women for that will be the end of our race."

La Llorona is more than a folk tale or a ghost story. She is the incarnation of maternal pain and loss. As a child abandoned by her mother, as the daughter of an abandoned mother, as the mother of an abandoned child, I, too, am La Llorona.

4

THE MYSTERY OF SURVIVAL

When my mother left me in the Colonia La Gran María, I was ten years old, and I hated men. My stepfather had once told me that women were like the earth, and that men could mine them and take anything they wanted. Girls, he said, especially ones like me who talked backed and disobeyed, had to be dealt with in a special way. I remember that evening like a deep secret I must never tell. My mother had gone to the orphanage with food and some of my old clothes.

"I'm not a woman," I cried, terrified staring down at the thing sticking out of his pants.

"You're a bad girl!" he told me, spanking me hard. "Men have to punish bad girls." He spanked me again and made me take it in my mouth. Later, when my mother came home, he went to the kitchen and told her I could no longer stay in his house.

"He doesn't love you. We can't live here anymore," my mother said as we walked to the plaza. "We're going away. To *la frontera*. To my cousin Lucía's house."

"Is your cousin Lucía married, Mamá?" I asked.

"She works on the other side. Maybe she can find me a job," she said. She had not heard my question.

In the plaza, we found an empty bench near the *kiosko*, and Mamá told me to sit with my back to her so that she could re-braid my hair with the new ribbons she had bought me.

"Why does he do those things to me, Mamá?"

She unwound my hair and combed it out with her fingers. "Remember, *hija*," she said at length, "the mystery of survival is obedience. If we can obey even the most terrible thing, we will survive it. If we disobey, we will always lose. Remember that. Obey and you will survive. Disobey and you will suffer."

"But it hurts me, sometimes, what he does."

"You think you hurt now, *hija*," she said, starting on the second braid. "Later you'll know that you survived. Later you'll know what real suffering is."

I watched the pigeons and the doves that lined the railing of the *kiosko*. Do birds have to obey? I wondered.

"Come on," Mamá said after she'd finished fixing my hair. "I'll buy you an *elote*. Do you want one?" We walked over to the man who was selling boiled corn on the cob slathered with mayonnaise. My stomach heaved.

"I'd rather have coconut," I said, and we went to the lady slicing coconut flesh on a cart.

"Everything on it," I said to the lady, and I watched her squeeze a lime over some slices in a plastic glass, powder them with red *chile* and sprinkle them with salt. The lady handed me the glass, and Mamá paid her from a little bag she wore between her breasts.

"Have you ever been to *la frontera*?" I asked as we strolled around the plaza eating coconut. Her eyes were shadowed. She did not want to speak.

We left the next morning. The sun had not risen yet, but women were already out sweeping their sidewalks and talking with the men who picked up the trash. I had to carry my clothes and my schoolbooks in a plastic market bag imprinted with the image of the Virgen de Guadalupe. Mamá lugged an old suitcase. She seemed strangely happy. She was shivering, from the cold, she said, but there was something about her face that I had never seen before. The line between her eyebrows wasn't pleated; her lips weren't pressed together as usual. She had parted her hair differently, and for once, I noticed the soft curve of her jawline, undisturbed by the constant flexing and unflexing of her jaw muscles that was her habit.

"You look beautiful, Mamá," I told her, slipping my free arm around her waist as we walked to the church. She stroked my cheek, then pressed me tightly to her side.

"My cousin Lucía is very nice," she said. "You're going to be happy, I know."

I narrowed my eyes. Was Mamá planning to send me off by myself? Or was she going to leave me with this cousin of hers the way she'd left me with her sister two years ago? Maybe she was coming back to live with him. I turned my head and saw him standing by the open window, tucking his shirt into his open pants.

"Will you stay with me?" I asked, keeping my voice low so that she wouldn't hear the fear in it.

"I *am* with you, *hija*. I will always be with you, no matter how far apart we are."

I could smell the starch in her dress and saw that she had worn her new shoes, the ones that she said hurt her when she walked. The market bag felt suddenly too heavy for me. I turned my face toward her body and cried into the dark cloth of her dress. The bells of Santa Clara tolled for the five-thirty Mass, and Mamá turned onto the street that led to the church, digging her mantilla out of her purse.

"Wait for me here," she said outside the entrance, leaving her suitcase beside me. I watched her go down the aisle, genuflect in front of the altar and turn left where the larger picture of the Virgen of Guadalupe hung in its golden frame. She lit a long candle and then knelt and made the triple sign of the cross over her face, heart and shoulders. The smell of incense and wax filtered out to me.

"It's bad luck to stand in the doorway of a church," said Don Anastacio, our next-door neighbor, who always attended early Mass before opening his shoe repair shop on the plaza. "What are you doing here so early, anyway?"

I didn't answer, just moved over to let him pass and decided to wait for Mamá further down the steps. Before leaving the churchyard, we stopped at the fountain where Mamá tossed an American coin into the water. She bought me five bags of pumpkin seeds from a man with no legs and told me to save them for the trip.

"We have to hurry," she said. "We still don't have our tickets."

She was going with me. I felt my stomach unclench. She hailed a taxi and haggled with him for a good price to the train station.

In the pink and gold of the sunrise, the town looked different to me. I had never realized how beautiful Querétaro was in the spring. The flowering jacaranda trees along Los Arcos were nearly as high as the arches of the aqueduct, casting a lavender glow on the thoroughfare all the way to the center of town and filling the streets with purple petals. The different-colored houses with potted geraniums on their balconies. The bells of all the churches ringing for morning Mass. The bright skirts of the Otomí women selling their embroidered cloths and blouses outside the train station. Inside the station, two boys wanted to carry our things. Mamá gave them each a bag of pumpkin seeds, and they ran off.

"Stay close to me," Mamá said as we stood in line to get our tickets to Ciudad Juárez.

Our train pulled out of Querétaro just as the big smelter sounded the morning horn. My stepfather would be leaving the house with his hard hat and the *lonchera* Mamá had prepared for him last night. Yesterday at this hour, Mamá was listening to the radio as she finished ironing my uniform. I was eating my breakfast and trying to memorize the paragraph on snakes in my biology book that I had to recite today at school. She told me not to tell anybody, not my teachers or my friends, that we were leaving.

Sitting on the cracked black seat of the moving train, I knew that I would never come back here. I would never go to that school again or wear that uniform. I understood then that the same thing that happened to snakes could happen to people.

Just outside the city limits of Querétaro, the train passed a long, whitewashed wall painted with the election messages of the PRI and PAN, and beside them, a proverb in green spray-painted letters that spelled out: El PUEBLO QUE PIERDE SU MEMORIA PIERDE SU DESTINO.

I asked Mamá what it meant.

"I don't know," she said, staring straight ahead and clutching her rosary beads as the train lurched. "Mexican proverbs don't mean anything anymore."

I looked out the window and tried to memorize the shape of the Cerro de las Campanas, the Hill of Bells, where a bronze Benito Juárez stood twenty meters into the sky. The same hill where Maximilian had one faced the firing squad on *cinco de mayo*. Did they have Cinco de Mayo parades in Ciudad Juárez, I wondered.

The rocking of the train lulled me to sleep almost immediately. We were sitting in second class, and the stench of the toilets was turning my stomach, so Mamá covered my face with her *rebozo* and told me to go to sleep.

"Be grateful we're not in third class," Mama said.

"*¿Hasta dónde van?*" the lady across the aisle from us asked.

"*A la frontera,*" Mamá said. "*Ciudad Juárez.*"

"*¡Híjole, se les va a hacer bien largo!*" said the lady. "But at least it's not as far as Tijuana. I went from DF to Tijuana, once, and I wanted to throw myself from the train halfway through." The lady laughed loud.

Mamá sighed and turned her face to the window. She did not want to talk anymore.

"The worst part is these trains are putrid, *todos podridos*, especially back here," the lady continued. "Just pray we don't get any passengers with pigs and goats."

"How long is it going to take us?" I mumbled under Mamá's *rebozo*.

"*Duérmete*," Mamá said, stroking my hair with her long nails until I fell asleep. When I opened my eyes hours later, the train was pulling into another station. The chatty lady was gone.

"*¿Ya llegamos?*" I asked, rubbing the sleep out of my eyes.

"We're just in Aguascalientes," Mamá said. "I hope you're not going to keep asking me that at every stop." She waved her hand in front of her to indicate how far down the line we still needed to go. "*Faltan dos días, todavía.* Here, have a *torta* before it goes bad. I saved you some of my *tamarindo* soda."

Two days to go? I thought. Maybe that's why that lady said she had wanted to throw herself from the train. Maybe I did, too.

I ate my *huevo con chorizo torta* that Mamá had made for the trip and took small sips of her flat soda, staring out the window at the names of the stations we passed: Zacatecas, Gómez Palacio, Parral, Camargo, Delicias—each one drier and uglier than the last. People of all ages climbed on and off with their roped boxes and cages of chickens and coolers full of sodas and food to sell—burritos, tacos and quesadillas. By the time we reached the Chihuahua station, two days later, we had to wait almost five hours for the train's toilets to get repaired.

Nearly three days and three nights after we left Querétaro, we finally stepped down onto the smelly platform of the train station in Ciudad Juárez. My belly felt swollen and queasy, and we were instantly swallowed into a bustling crowd. Mamá held my hand tightly as she tried to maneuver us and our bags through that river of bodies. Some of them did not smell so good. Or maybe it was just me that stunk after three days of not washing or changing my underwear.

Finally, outside, a taxi driver offered to carry our bags, and Mamá told him the name of the *colonia* we were going to. The man shook his head and told us that taxis didn't go into the *colonias*. Too dangerous, he said, dropping our bags at our feet. No paved streets. For that, we would have to take a *rutera*, and he pointed to a white van that was just leaving the station.

"Take the one that says '*colonias*,'" the man called behind us as we stepped out. "And don't take your eyes off your bags. There's always *maleantes* on those things looking for easy prey."

The *rutera* stuffed what looked like twenty of us inside, even though the sign painted on the door said there was room for only fifteen passengers. I looked out the grimy mud and bird-shit splattered window and tried to breathe. Mamá did not tell me we were coming to a place as ugly as this, where there were beggars on every corner and more trash than trees. The *rutera* zigzagged through long lines of traffic and crossed the railroad tracks just before a cargo train whistled by.

Mamá asked the woman bending over her if the driver was crazy.

"They don't care," the woman said. "They're human beasts. *¿De a dónde vienen?* Are you from the south?" "

"From Querétaro," Mamá said. "My daughter and I are looking for the Colonia La Gran María."

"La Gran María?" the woman repeated, shaking her head. "Never heard of it. Does anybody know where this Colonia Gran María is?" she asked everyone in the vehicle.

"That's the last stop," the driver said over his shoulder.

The woman made a strange face, pulling her mouth down and her head back, eyes rolling like she had just heard some bad news.

The *rutera* stopped suddenly behind a bus, and the woman and a few other passengers squeezed out. Ahead of us I could see

I looked at Mamá and Mamá nodded.

"No," I said. "I'm thirsty."

"Who isn't?" Lucía said, standing up again and reaching for my market bag. "Everything is thirsty in the desert." She took Mamá's suitcase as well.

"She's being a Mrs. Contreras right now," Mamá told Lucía. "If I say good, she'll say bad. If I say food, she'll say water."

I stayed behind them as we walked in the direction of one of the shacks. It was made of mismatched planks of lumber and had a corrugated tin roof and a striped sarape hanging in the doorway. Suddenly, a white dog bounded out from behind a heap of old tires. Mamá screamed. Lucía whistled sharply, and the dog slowed down.

"This is Sancho," Lucía said when the dog was beside me, sniffing my knees. "Don't be afraid of him. He's a good friend."

I had never touched a white dog, and his fur felt strangely soft, strangely clean in this dusty place. He stood there patiently while I petted his back and scratched between his pink-tipped ears.

"Don't worry," Lucía told Mamá as they moved on, "my father whipped all the wildness out of him.

Her father? I thought. Does Mamá's cousin Lucía have a man in her house? The mask of my stepfather's face fell over the dog's head. Eyes bloodshot. Teeth bared. You're a bad girl! Men have to punish bad girls. Get the devil out of them. Clean the devil out with this. Swallow it! Swallow it!

Sharp needles were pushing into my head. My mouth tasted of vomit. Faraway, I heard my mother's voice.

"She hardly ate anything on the train," she was saying.

I heard swishing water, then something sticky and wet covered my forehead. It smelled of melon.

"She's waking up," said another voice, closer. My eyes cracked open.

"Also, maybe it was the heat." Mamá sounded old.

I heard the squeaking of bedsprings, and then I was helped to sit up, my head resting on an unknown hand. The wet thing on my forehead fell off me, and I saw that it was a cantaloupe rind.

"Drink this, *hija*."

Hot liquid touched my lips. The smell of chicken broth woke me completely. I was lying on a box spring in a room with no windows, the afternoon light arrowing in through the cracks in the walls. A cot with a thin mattress and a pillow stood in the corner. Two crates pushed up against a table served as chairs. On another crate, an altar had been assembled, crowded with framed pictures of saints, including a soldier saint I had never seen, little statues of *la Virgen*, San Martin de Porres and San Judas, votive candles, a jar of dark liquid and a tin cup with feathers in it. The glow of the candles flickered on the dirt floor.

I was gulping the broth down more quickly than Mamá could spoon it out of the bowl, and Lucía told me that I was going to make myself sick again if I ate so fast.

"I'm hungry," I told her, remembering suddenly that she had a man in her house, a man who probably slept in that cot over there in this one-room hovel.

I pulled away from Lucía and told Mamá that I didn't want to stay here, that I was afraid of that man in this house, that he would do what the other man had done.

Mamá stopped feeding me, her face slowly darkening to a deep red. "Can you give us a moment?" she said to her cousin, gesturing with her head that she wanted her to leave the room.

Quietly, Lucía left, taking the half-finished bowl of soup with her. When she had gone, and the sarape flapped over the doorway again, Mamá turned to me and slapped me hard.

"You must never talk about that!" she hissed. "If you do, La Llorona will come to you. She'll drag you to the river and drown you."

I bent my head to one side, eyes narrowed. "That's not true, that's just *puro cuento*," I said, rubbing the burn of her hand on my face. "And there aren't any rivers around here, anyway."

"This is *la frontera*," Mamá said. "El Rio Grande is right behind us. When you wake up one night and hear La Llorona calling you from the river, you'll see if her story is true or not."

"She doesn't know my name," I said, tracing the lines in my skirt.

"La Llorona knows all the Mexican children. I've told you that." She paused for a moment, and her eyes flattened like the ears of an angry cat. "She was there when you were born!"

The look in her eyes made me wet my pants a little. I was afraid it would show on my skirt if I got up.

"I'm not afraid," I told her, lying back down.

I covered myself with the threadbare sheet and pretended to sleep. She stayed beside me a long time afterwards, mumbling to herself that same monotonous sound that meant she was praying. Then, she bent over me and made the sign of the cross over my face, pressing her thumb to my mouth for the Amen.

"Mamá?" I whispered. "Do you love him more than me?"

She stroked my back. "How can you ask me that?" she said. "I didn't mean to hit you so hard. You embarrassed me in front of Lucía."

"How long do we have to stay here?"

She did not answer right away. Her hand kept stroking me, and I could feel the numbness of sleep spreading down my spine. Finally, she spoke. "I'm going to try to cross over tonight," she said. "Lucía tells me they are hiring at the university. I'll be close by. Right across the river in those buildings we saw."

"That's a university?" I said, my eyes sinking deeper and deeper into sleep.

"I'll take you to the movies every Sunday, just like I used to in Querétaro. And I'll bring you story books in English. Doña Inés can teach you how to read them. By the time you're fifteen,

I'll have my green card, and we can live together on the other side."

"Who's Doña Inés?" I was barely awake.

She bent over me again and kissed my cheek. "Go to sleep. Lucía will tell you all about Doña Inés later." She kissed me again, then got up and was gone.

A hot breeze swirled into the room. A branch rattled against the side of the shack. The wet spot had started to sting, and I thought it would be a good idea to take off my skirt and let it dry in the breeze, but I was too numb to move. I closed my eyes and was already asleep when I heard someone coming into the room. For one terrible instant, I thought it was Lucía's father. I clenched my fists and my eyes, but then something cold pressed against the back of my neck. It was only Sancho sniffing at this stranger in his house. I heard him flop down beside the bed, a deep yawn coming from his mouth. *Good friend*, I thought over and over.

I must have slept for hours because when I awoke, it was night, and a kerosene lamp had been lit on the table. Everything in the room looked huge with shadow. I sat up suddenly, for a moment not knowing where I was. Then I noticed that Mamá's suitcase was open, and her clothes were gone. I jumped out of the tangled bedsheet and tore outside.

Lucía and an old man were sitting on a pile of old tires in front of a stove made of bricks and a piece of tin. The air smelled of woodsmoke and hot corn. Lucía stood up as I approached.

"Papá, here she is," she said to him.

The old man stared at the tortillas warming on the tin and nodded his head.

"*Bienvenida a la orilla del mundo*," he said, not looking up. Beside him, Sancho thumped his tail on the dirt. Mamá was not there.

"Everybody calls my father Tito," Lucía said.

"Where's my mother?" I asked, nearly spitting the words at her.

"The coyote was crossing everyone tonight, since there's no moon," Lucía explained, pointing down in the direction of the river. "She wanted to let you rest. She said to tell you to be strong and to send her good luck so that she gets that job."

"When is she coming back?"

The old man raised his face to look at me, and I saw that he was ancient and that his eyes were white with cataracts. The fear of Lucía's father slipped out of me like a gas.

"She will stay there until she has enough money to come and get you," he said. "Until then, you will live with us, and Lucía will take care of you."

A fist suddenly formed in my throat. I could not see the river, only the headlights of the cars on the two highways and the bright windows of the university where Mamá had said she would be working. I imagined standing on the riverbank, looking up, trying to find Mamá's face in one of those windows. I remembered the way I had once looked for the face of Benito Juárez on the statue on the Hill of Bells that stretched so high above Querétaro, its face was sometimes hidden in the clouds.

"*Vamos*," Lucía said, picking up an old flashlight and wrapping a few tortillas in a frayed cloth. "Let's go take these to Doña Inés. She's waiting to meet you."

"Who's Doña Inés?"

"She's our *curandera*," said Lucía, lighting the dirt road in front of us.

Above me, the sky was so dark the stars glittered like shiny sand. On the way, a girl about my age joined us.

"*Hola*, Lucy," the girl said to Lucía, reaching out for her hand.

"*¿Qué tal?* Mi'ja."

The girl grinned at me. "My name is Guillermina, but everyone calls me Mina," she said, "What's your name?"

"Xochitl," I said, staring at her cleft lip. "What happened to your mouth?"

"My father says the devil kissed me when I was born, but Doña Inés says that's a lie. She says some kids are born like this, and I can have it operated when I grow up."

"Does it hurt?" I asked.

"Not at all," said Mina, "do you want to feel it?"

"Doña Inés is teaching Mina how to read and write in English," said Lucía, pulling me away before I could touch Mina's face. "She lives up here in her school."

We climbed up a steep dark alley that smelled of urine and wet earth. At the top stood a little adobe house surrounded by a fence of sunflowers and thorny ocotillos. On a wooden sign nailed to a stake in front of the house, it said: GRAMMARYE SCHOOL/ESCUELA LA GRAN MARIA.

"Can I learn English, too?" I asked.

"Of course," said Lucía. "You're going to need it when you cross over to *el otro lado*."

"She teaches magic, *también*," said Mina. "When my sister disappeared, she showed me how to bring her back."

5

MUJERES NECIAS / DECOLONIAL FEMINISTS UNITE!

Dorothy Schons and Sor Juana Inés de la Cruz

Unlike my cousins growing up on the Mexican side of the El Paso/Juárez border, I did not learn about Sor Juana in my English-only Catholic elementary schools, much less memorize her famous "Political Satire" on "*hombres necios que acusáis/a la mujer sin razón.*"[1] My cousins, my uncles and their wives, my father and grandfather, even my grandmother with her second-grade education—everyone seemed to know this poem, or at least the first couple of quatrains, by heart. As a budding organic feminist in high school, I was fascinated that a 17th-century nun could write such a strong critique of patriarchy and its double-standards. Who was this nun? What had happened in her life that led her to pen those brazen lines that blamed men for the faults and sins they, themselves, solicited from women? Ten years would pass before I could begin the research that would help me answer those questions.

Back in 1986, when Sor Juana Inés de la Cruz first started speaking to me in my dreams, I would be talking to her on the phone—that old rotary black phone my grandparents used to have. I could see her clearly, wearing her black and white Hieronymite habit and my black wingtips. I had the same dream enough times to know that my subconscious was trying to tell me

something. Was Sor Juana walking in my shoes, or was I supposed to in-habit her life? That we were on the phone clearly
meant she was trying to communicate with me. With a Master of
Arts degree in English–Creative Writing, I had my heart set on
becoming a novelist, and had been intrigued by Sor Juana since
I was a child, listening in rapt wonder to my uncles and cousins
reciting her "*hombres necios*" poem.

Maybe the dream was telling me that I had to write a novel
on Sor Juana, that I had to filter her story as a colonial Mexican
nun/poet/scholar (symbolized by her habit) through my vision as
a late-20th-century Chicana lesbian writer (symbolized by my
wingtips). At the time, I was living in exile from academia. I had
started my Ph.D. in American Studies at the University of Iowa
in Fall 1985, but after two semesters, I became disenchanted, not
with Iowa City or the community of queer Latinidad I had found
there, but with the field itself, and with the whiteness of the program, its jargon stultifying and meaningless to the activist work
I saw myself doing in the academy. I moved back to El Paso to
regroup, but soon discovered I had to leave home for good if I
ever expected to live my own examined and independent life.

My Argentinian girlfriend with whom I'd hooked up in Iowa
City had gotten accepted to UMASS/Boston, and I followed her,
figuring that New England would be a great place to be a writer.
Living in Boston, I learned about public transportation, T stations
underground that reeked of urine while beside and across from
me on the train, people had their faces buried in a book or a newspaper. Walking all over the Back Bay, up and down Boyle Street
to and from The Public Library, the Common and the Public Garden, I learned about the unhoused. In El Paso and Iowa City I
had never seen so many people—of all ages and races—living
their lives out in the open, regardless of the weather. They were
everywhere, what Emma Lazarus in her poem at the foot of the
Statue of Liberty called "the poor and the homeless tempest tost"
to the cold shores of the East Coast: not just the public places,

but the Museum of Fine Art, the Isabella Gardener Museum, Faneul Hall, Copley Square, the School of Music. Not just McDonald's but Au Bon Pain. Big city life, I guess.

There was one couple whom we called Hector and Angela, who hung out in the park across the street from our apartment on The Fenway, and who were always fighting late into the night. Sometimes the fights got really ugly, and she would show up alone near the Green Line stop on Mass Ave. with a huge bruise on the side of her face. At night, they'd be together again, huddled under a blanket, passing a bottle between them. Once, on my daily walk back from The Trident bookstore on Marlborough Street, she looked me right in the eye as I passed, and said "I'm nobody, but I'm still somebody." She was not asking for money; she was asking for respect.

Something else that opened my eyes. Surrounded by white people with Boston accents, as well as people of color from all over the world, I discovered that most of them had never even heard the word *Chicana*, much less understood its history or its function as an identity. It was easier to call myself Mexican, even if it did make me seem like an immigrant to the United States. At least, being an immigrant was something the people I interacted with understood. This new-fangled identity named Chicana was much more alien to them than Mexican.

The Latinos and Latinas I met all had different accents, and soon my Spanish became inflected with Cuban, Puerto Rican and Argentinian expressions like "ya tu sabes," "no jodas, chica," or "Che, cariño." Who needed a Ph.D., when I had humanity to teach me everything I needed to know about difference and multiculturalism? I already had a Master's degree; I didn't need a doctorate, or so the right side of my brain rationalized. I needed trees, culture and emotional stability, not boring readings on theory and methodology. Besides, I told myself, it made sense for me to live in New England, where I would be closer to the publishing industry, and perhaps even get an editorial job at a literary press.

The closest I came to working in the publishing industry was my job as a transcriber of books for the blind at the National Braille Press, walking distance from my apartment in the Back Bay. Learning Braille as a sighted person was fun for the first three months, but the full-time job ended up being even more numbing to my creative brain than academic jargon. After a year of 9 to 5 drudgery and coming home bleary-eyed after my long shift reading reliefs of Braille dots on a white page, I ended up getting diagnosed with depression. My doctor prescribed anti-depressants (which I never took), and then I learned I had a growth on my thyroid that was probably causing some of that emotional turmoil. I also learned one of the most important lessons of my writing life: that time is a non-renewable commodity, that you can always make up money, but you can never make up time. There was no way I was going to live the writer's life if I didn't make time for it. So, I downgraded my hours at the Braille Press to a part-time schedule, afternoons only, dedicating myself to transcribing children's books, and got a part-time teaching job in the English Department at UMASS/Boston. I invested $600 in a used IBM Selectric typewriter and committed to a writing life. Every morning, I would put on some Mercedes Sosa or Silvio Rodríguez music, light a stick of Nag Champa incense, and sit at my makeshift desk with a stack of colored scratch paper to give myself over to writing the Great Chicana Novel.[2]

There were two topics that fascinated me as potential subjects for that novel: Sor Juana Inés de la Cruz and the Salem witchcraft trials. Since I had chosen Boston as my residence and lived a few blocks away from the Boston Public Library, I figured it would make sense to write a novel on the witch trials, first, as it would be much easier to access research and archival materials about that subject than about Sor Juana. And yet, I couldn't get Sor Juana out of my mind. She spoke to me constantly. Why was this nun so insistent? From the small amount of research I had done on Sor Juana, and her image on the old $1000 Mexican peso note that I carried in my wallet and couldn't stop looking at—a nun in her habit sitting at her desk surrounded by books—I knew we shared some commonalities. Writing. A passion for books. A rebellious feminist streak that made us question and challenge gendered double standards in patriarchy. A love of women, perhaps? How could I connect her story to the Salem witch trials?

One afternoon, while sweeping my apartment, listening to a cassette of Hildegard of Bingen's ethereal chants for nuns' voices (Gregorian Chants had not become a hip musical genre yet), it came to me, the connective thread between these narratives: the year, 1692. That year is almost synonymous with, or rather synecdochous, of one of the most egregious misogynistic moments in American history, when a certain sector of the female population in New England, and the few men who supported them, were targets of a massive witch hunt, accused by their neighbors, their magistrates, and their ministers (sometimes by their own children) of bewitching anybody who crossed their paths, blighting crops, dancing in the woods naked and signing the Devil's book. Starting in March 1692, with the arrest and incarceration of a Barbados slave named Tituba, the accused (mostly women) were dragged into filthy, freezing jail cells in Boston, Salem, and throughout the Commonwealth of Massachusetts, to await their trials or their turn at the gallows. So many were accused that by summertime, the jails overflowed with witches, all their goods and possessions confiscated by their town courts. In September, 22 women were hung and one man pressed to death with heavy stones for refusing to confess their sin of trafficking with the Devil.

To my knowledge, Sor Juana was never accused of being a witch, even though she did come perilously close to having her soul excommunicated by the Catholic Church. But Sor Juana *was* alive in 1692, quickly moving toward her life's denouement three years later and beginning to pay the price for her uncanny intelligence, her powers of rhetoric and poetry, her recalcitrant disobedience of her vows and her superiors. 1692 was also a bad year for New Spain. A long drought followed by torrential rains, epidemics of smallpox and cholera, blighted corn, hunger and riots characterized Mexico City, and the archbishop ordered the religious of all the convents in the city to increase their prayers and intensify their mortifications of the flesh in a concerted effort to appeal to the mercy of the Heavenly Father.

What if, I wondered, somehow, these two seventeenth-century narratives in North America could be experienced at the same time, a literary sort of quantum physics in which these parallel plot lines could unravel in separate sections of the novel—New Spain and New England—and then converge somehow in the awful events of 1692? Considering that I'd never actually written a historical novel, that was one mind-boggling premise, far above my pay grade as a part-time author, English-as-a-Second-Language instructor, Braille transcriber. That's when the Sor Juana dreams doubled down. She didn't offer me any clear directions on how to begin writing this Hydra of a story, but her persistent apparition in my dreams—dare I say, she haunted me?—kept my unconscious busy.

That day in 1986 when I was sweeping my apartment, I conceived of the whole story. From start to finish, in one flash of a second, I saw that the way to connect these colonial narratives would be with one character—an immigrant servant in Boston accused of witchcraft. What is she being accused of? Speaking in tongues (i.e., Spanish), practicing the Popish custom of making the sign of the cross over her face and praying to a craven image (i.e., an embroidery of the Virgin of Guadalupe), teaching her young daughter the "Devil's verse."

Unlike most of the servants in New England, this immigrant girl is literate. She can read and write and work arithmetic. She has uncanny calligraphy skills and supposedly curses folks with her forked tongue and her two-colored eyes. The so-called Devil's verse that she is trying to teach her daughter is Sor Juana's famous "Hombres Necios" poem, which ends with Sor Juana's judgement that men embody "world, flesh, and Devil." It's Sor Juana's "Philosophical Satire" on gender double-standards and the nefarious male practice of blaming women for men's wrongdoing that this servant, half-indigenous, half-Spanish (a mestiza in racial parlance) is overheard speaking, which gets her fingered for a witch.[3]

The broom dropped to the hardwood floor. I ran to the typewriter to compose the idea, fingers flying over the black Selectric keys like one possessed. At that moment, it did not matter that writing such a story was going to take a copious amount of research, let alone time, to complete. Who was this mestiza? What was her name? How had a mestiza gotten to New England in the first place? Who was her daughter? And the most important question of all, why was she quoting Sor Juana? Would this be Sor Juana's story or the mestiza's? Or were these supposed to be two separate stories after all? Maybe I had to write the New England story with the mestiza, first, and then the second book could be Sor Juana's story in New Spain. Or vice versa. Talk about complicating yourself into a literary corner.

I decided to start in New England, with the mestiza's story, whom I named Concepción, for it was through her that I conceived of this complex storyline. Not only would Concepción be able to remember—and hence, flashback—to her life in New Spain with Sor Juana, but also, she would be right there during the witch hunts, our guide through the madness created by another breed of misogynistic *hombres necios*. Besides, research materials on colonial New England and the witch craze were plentiful at the Boston Library. Every morning when I wasn't commuting to the UMASS/Boston campus to teach English-as-a-Second-Language courses to immigrant students from Africa, China and Latin America, I would pack all my research materials into a surplus-green canvas backpack and walk the twenty minutes that it took me from the Back Bay to the Boston Library. Perusing drawers of library cards looking for the subject areas Boston History, Early New England, Pirates and Witchcraft, I managed to locate and collect stacks of books that I hauled over to an empty table and sat down to research. I struck gold almost immediately, as in one of the Boston histories I found an article about the buccaneer economy in New England, through which sugar, rum and slaves came to be traded and sold in the Boston port. In a footnote in that article, I read about a 17th-century Dutch buccaneer (the polite word for pirate among the Puritans) named Laurens de Graf, who liked to plunder the Spanish Main, what we now call the Pacific and Atlantic oceans around Mexico and the Caribbean.

In May of the year 1683, Laurens de Graf, known in Mexico as Lorencillo, the Scourge of New Spain, greatly feared for the terrible crimes he perpetrated on the communities he put under siege while his company raped and pillaged to its hearts' content, besieged the port of San Juan de Ulloa in Veracruz while the Spanish galleons carrying gold and other precious resources from the Americas back to Spain sat like brooding hens in the harbor, unable to stop the ransack. There it was! The literal vehicle by which Concepción gets transported between New Spain and New England—the ship of Lorencillo. This same pirate whom the godly New England merchants did business with as a buccaneer transported a lucrative trade in sugar and slaves to the New England coast. Was it a coincidence that Sor Juana had written a piece called "Neptuno alegórico" to welcome her beloved Condesa and her Viceroy husband to Mexico City in 1680 and that the pirate ship Concepcion boards in Veracruz three years later is called *The Neptune?* As a Jungian, I don't believe in coincidences. I won't reveal what happens on the journey. Suffice it to say that this young mixed-race literate woman, trained as a scribe by the great Mexican intellectual, Sor Juana Inés de la Cruz, is sold as a slave to a New England merchant, her memory full of Sor Juana's verses, her body impregnated by Laurens de Graf.

ᎶᏧᎀ ᎶᏧᎀ ᎶᏧᎀ

"You want to write a novel about what?" Sor Juana asks, peering over the tiny reading glasses affixed to the end of her nose.

"How a mestiza who was captured in New Spain by pirates, transported to New England and sold as a slave in Boston, gets accused of witchcraft for speaking in tongues and pronouncing the words of your 'Political Satire' on *hombres necios.*"

Sor Juana frowns but her hazel eyes shift quickly back and forth as if tabulating the value of such a story. "Who was this mestiza?"

"Your scribe, who makes copies of your work in a beautiful calligraphy, who memorized the poem before she ran away from the convent and got captured by pirates."

"Captured by pirates? That reminds me of a story by my friend, Don Carlos."

"Yes, 'The Adventures of Alonso Ramírez.' I read it."

"Did you? Will your mestiza be stowing away on a ship?"

I still hadn't figured out how Concepción would come aboard Lorencillo's ship. Stowing away might not be a bad idea.

"Of course, you wouldn't want to repeat Don Carlos' idea."

"Of course not!" I say, embarrassed the thought crossed my mind for a nano-second.

"She's a mestiza, you say?"

"Actually, she's more of a castiza, the daughter of a *china poblana* and a criollo—her mother is a mix of Spanish, African, Filipina and Indigenous blood, and her father is of Spanish descent."

"Is this daughter of a *china poblana* a maid in the convent?"

"Yes and no. She's the illegitimate granddaughter of the Mother Superior, and her father has indentured her service to the convent for twenty years."

A thin smile creases Sor Juana's lips. "Yes, that happened quite frequently with illegitimate daughters."

I realize she's alluding discreetly to her own situation. Born a "natural" daughter of the Church, a euphemism for illegitimate, she, too, was placed in the Convent of Santa Paula, not as a maid, but a sister of the Order of Saint Jerome, her body and soul indentured to the convent until her death.

"And the Mother Superior assigns her to you to assist you with your work."

"Obviously, this is a fictional treatment not a biographical one, since I never had a scribe or an assistant."

"I like to use fiction to convey truths that can't be told otherwise."

"Well, you have my blessing, but I have one request," she says, "no, not a request, a condition: that you not paint me as a girl genius or a religious martyr but, as I say in my 'Respuesta a Sor Filotea,' as a woman struggling to learn not for celebrity or self-indulgence, but for the sake of lessening my own ignorance."[4]

"A struggle against the *hombres necios* of the Church who wanted to control your mind as well as your body, and your own unquenchable desire to acquire knowledge and exercise your free will," I say, finishing her sentence.

"That wasn't my only unquenchable desire," she says, winking.

"I know. That's why I'm writing this book. And because I want to explore why in your lifetime you were called 'the phoenix of Mexico' and '*la décima musa.*' Why, in my lifetime, you are hailed as the 'first feminist of the Americas.'"

"It's so tedious to have to live up to all these epithets," Sor Juana says, shaking her head, returning her eyes to her reading.

"But yes, you'll find what you're looking for in my scribblings. You'll have to read between the lines, read the silences and the omissions, since I wasn't free to write everything that I truly wanted to say. Many years ago, my devoted American friend, Dorothy Schons, started to write my story, but she had difficulties and never finished it. Maybe you will finish yours."

෴ ෴ ෴

At first, I paid no attention to the name of Dorothy Schons. Sor Juana had given me a mission. Before I could write about her, before I could even imagine writing in her voice and from her point of view, I had to read Sor Juana's work, not just the English translations of her work, but the original baroque Spanish that she used for her poetry, her prose and her plays. Don't get me wrong—I devoured the English translations as well, otherwise I would still be navigating the high seas of Sor Juana's wordplay and rhetoric. But I also had to research the colonial history, the racial politics, the daily culture of seventeenth-century New Spain. Indeed, I had to learn everything I could about cloistered life in a colonial convent, about Sor Juana's process of becoming a nun, her years as a girl-scholar and then a lady-in-waiting at the viceregal court, her relationships with her peers and her superiors, with her sisters and her mother and her grandfather, her disagreements with the other nuns, the priests who supported and attacked her, and most especially, her intimate friendships with two vicereines. Not to mention all the other minutiae that constitutes a historical novel.

Those were the days of no Internet, no Google, no Wikipedia, no YouTube, no open-access research materializing on the screen with the click of a button. In fact, there were no screens, no computers, no passwords, and research meant slogging through drawers of Dewey decimal reference cards to find the titles I was looking for, walking the stacks to locate the needed books and perusing the shelves for any useful surprises. It was a surprise, in fact, that I found any sources relating to Sor Juana at the Boston Public Library, but my tenacity yielded some valuable preliminary results, such as a copy of Francisco de la Maza's *Sor Juana Inés de la Cruz ante la historia*, volume I of Alfonso Méndez Plancarte's edited series Sor Juana's *Obras Completas*, and Octavio Paz's *Sor Juana, o Las trampas de la fe*, all in Spanish, and in English, Irving Leonard's *Baroque Times in Old Mexico* and Gerard Flynn's *Sor Juana Inés de la Cruz*. I also found a few articles that I was able to locate via interlibrary loan.

By pure serendipity, I was invited to read my poetry at a Latino literature conference in San Antonio, Texas, where I met Margaret Sayers Peden, translator par excellence of the most iconic Latin American literature, including Sor Juana's poetry and Octavio Paz's *Traps of Faith*. The conference was connected to the International Hemispheric Book Fair, where at the booth of a random bookseller, I found three of the four volumes of Sor Juana's *Complete Works* (which I purchased for an unbelievable price of $60 total). It would take me a few years to locate the fourth volume on a dusty bottom shelf of a bookstore in downtown Mexico City. And then my mother gifted me with my own copy of Octavio Paz's magnum opus in the original Spanish.

My research bed was made, but now I had to sleep on it for a decade while I completed the PhD and secured a tenure-track job; only after submitting the manuscript that became my first academic book, which would eventually earn me a promotion with tenure at UCLA, was I able to return to Sor Juana and Concepción, assemble all the pieces I had written in the previous decade and reread the research I had done back in Boston. It was then that I met Dr. Dorothy Schons, a Latin Americanist scholar (and arguably the earliest *sorjuanista*) at the University of Texas, who in 1925, called Sor Juana "The First Feminist of the New Word."

Dorothy Schons, The Original *sorjuanista*

Unless you have gone to the Nettie Lee Benson Latin American Collection at The University of Texas at Austin and requested the Dorothy Schons Papers, you will have missed two of the most important documents of Sor Juana lore ever collected. The first is the more than 300-year-old *Libro de Profesiones*, or Book of Professions, of the Convent of Santa Paula in Mexico City, in which 350 novices over a period of more than a century inscribed their Testaments of Faith to enter life in religion as Hieronymite nuns. Why would Dorothy Schons have that convent's Book of Professions in her possession, the same one in which Sor Juana signed her vows to the Order of Saint Jerome? Was there some mistake? Was the book a facsimile? Was Sor Juana leading me inexorably to that archive so that I could see with my own eyes her famous signature in her own blood?

When I first set foot in the Benson as a graduate student in the early 1990s, it was possible to take the ancient book out of its archival box with your own gloved hands and study the original page on which Sor Juana first signed her vows to the convent in 1669, which she renewed 25 years later in her own blood. It was hard to see the "*la peor del mundo, la peor que ha habido*"[5] designation she gave herself at her vow-renewal, but if I squinted hard enough, I could make it out, her signature in that fading brown ink stain of dried blood in which she mortgaged her life and soul to the convent for the second and last time. I cannot say how long I stared at that page, but my hand was trembling as my palm hovered over the writing. I so much wanted to touch her dried blood with my own flesh. Catholic upbringing, you know.

The second fascinating discovery in the Schons archive is an incomplete original manuscript, most of the pages typewritten, a few in carbon copy, of the first English-language novel on Sor Juana, written by Dorothy Schons circa 1930 and titled, "Sor

Juana: A Chronicle of Old Mexico."[6] In the preface, Schons unequivocally situates Sor Juana's life within feminist history by
likening the nun's struggle to the suffragist cause: "Two hundred
years before Susan B. Anthony initiated the feminist movement
in this country, there appeared in the New World a woman who
was undoubtedly one of the earliest American Feminists. Strange
as it may seem, this woman was a Mexican nun."[7]

A few lines later, Schons segues from suffragist to decolonial feminist: "What [Sor Juana's] environment did to her, [is
what] Mexico's past has done to the Mexican people. . . . Mexico's plea for social justice arises out of social inequalities inherited from colonial times." Schons' novelized interpretation of Sor
Juana's life intended to show that patriarchy had conquered Sor
Juana as surely as the Spanish conquistadores colonized Mexico—leaving both collapsing under the social injustices wrought
by the greed and cruelty of *hombres necios.*

With such a visionary interpretation, why is it that the con-
tributions of Dorothy Schons to the *sorjuanista* canon are in fact
not considered canonical works except by those critics in the
fields of Golden Age Literature and Latin American Studies with
more feminist inclinations?[8] Because she was writing in the
1930s? Because she was a woman in academia at a time when
there were few pedigreed female professors? Because the patriarchal academy did not expect female professors to be "scholars" or visionaries, but to provide essential services to their
departments and universities such as grading papers, teaching
languages and composition, and assisting their male colleagues
with manuscript editing? Or was there something more sinister
going on, something that led to Professor Schons's suicide in
1961? What follows is a summary of "some obscure points"[9] on
the life of Dorothy Schons that might shed some light on why
this pioneering Sor Juana scholar all but disappeared under the
huge shadow of Octavio Paz and the Golden Age *sorjuanistas.*

Octavio Paz, The Seminal *sorjuanista*

Sor Juana Inés de la Cruz o Las trampas de la fe, Octavio Paz's magnum opus, then—and still—considered the ultimate resource on the seventeenth-century Mexican nun/scholar/poet, was particularly illuminating for my contextual research on New Spain—but not so much his literary interpretations of Sor Juana. It was in Paz's prologue that I first encountered a reference to one Dorothy Schons. In a very brief genealogy of twentieth-century scholars who have studied Sor Juana, apart from himself, Paz writes that *"[l]as últimas en llegar fueron las mujeres,"*[10] implying that women scholars and writers came late to the study of Sor Juana. First among them, he lists Dorothy Schons. He quotes Schons extensively throughout *Trampas de la fe*, and the footnotes at the bottom of the page reference Schons articles published in 1926, 1929 and 1934. Keep in mind that Octavio Paz's seminal essay on Sor Juana, "Homenaje a Sor Juana Inés de la Cruz en su tercer centenario (1651–1695),"[11] which generated his magnum opus, was not published until 1951, so I'm perplexed about why he would say that the last to arrive at the study of Sor Juana were the women scholars and writers, when his own first text came 25 years after Dorothy Schons's first publication!

To be fair, Paz credits Schons with writing the first *tentativa,* or attempt, at a feminist interpretation of Sor Juana by inserting Sor Juana's life and work into the misogynistic history of seventeenth-century New Spain: "La erudita norteamericana trató de comprender el feminismo de la poetisa como una reacción frente a la sociedad hispánica, su acentuada misoginia y su cerrado universo masculino."[12] And yet, in a manifestation of his own accentuated masculine ego, he discredits her authority by saying that unfortunately Schons never published more than two or three articles on Sor Juana, and not having published a book, all she left were a few *"atisbos aislados,"* or isolated inklings of an interpretation.

Book or not, he certainly availed himself generously of her research and her insights. I wonder why Paz chose not to cite Dorothy Schons's 1925 essay, "Sor Juana: The First Feminist of the New World,"[13] where she makes her argument for Sor Juana's proto-feminist standpoint quite clear and persuasive. There were reasons she never published a book on Sor Juana, which I will discuss later. Let me just reiterate here, that it was not Octavio Paz who baptized Sor Juana "the first feminist in the New World," but Miss Dorothy Schons, while still a PhD student, a full 25 years before Octavio Paz published his first essay on our "tenth muse."[14]

Surrender, Dorothy

Originally from Saint Paul, Minnesota, Dorothy Schons (1892–1961) taught in the Department of Romance Languages (now Spanish and Portuguese) at the University of Texas at Austin from 1919 to 1960. She earned her Bachelor of Arts degree at the University of Minnesota in 1912 (at age 20), started her Master of Arts degree at the University of Chicago, and then was hired as a Romance languages instructor at UT Austin. She completed the Master's in 1922 (at 30) and stayed on at UT Austin as a PhD student and an instructor in the department. In 1927 (at age 35), she ascended to the rank of Assistant Professor, and five years later, completed the requirements for her PhD (now, she's 40). It wasn't until 1943 (at 51 years of age) that she was promoted to Associate Professor without tenure. In 1960, when she was fired from the university, she was still not tenured, nor did she ever reach the rank of full professor. Was this the probable cause of that allegedly self-inflected bullet wound to the head a year later?

For a little historical context, we must recall that the 19th Constitutional amendment allowing women to vote did not become law until 1920. Indeed, Schons herself was a suffragist and a member of the National Woman's Party. As late as 1925, teachers in the Texas School District who got married automatically became property of their husbands, and so lost their contracts. In between Schons' promotion to Assistant Professor and her filing the dissertation that finally bestowed the PhD to her name, the Great Depression devastated the United States. Women en masse lost the jobs they had been recruited for during the first World War to accommodate more men back into the workforce. Socially, women were expected to resume their role as helpmeets of their husbands and caretakers of the home and family. A woman like Schons, unmarried, with a professional degree and a university teaching position, was as anomalous in post-World War I Texas as Sor Juana was in seventeenth-century New Spain.

After 41 years of labor and service to the University of Texas, after teaching thousands of students (including Georgina Sabat de Rivers, one of the most respected *sorjuanistas* in the field of Spanish letters), publishing six books and fifty articles on Hispanic literature, religious drama and the nuns of New Spain, and winning important academic accolades in Mexico and Spain, how is it fathomable that Dr. Schons did not get tenure? In *Dorothy Schons: La primera sorjuanista*, Guillermo Schmidhumer de la Mora observes that, given her expertise and decades of research on Sor Juana, it seems odd that the topic of Schons' dissertation was a male critic of Mexican comedy; he makes an informed guess that "perhaps her professors frowned on the practice of a woman researching another woman during a time in which Sor Juana's fame as a literary and human figure had not yet become consolidated."[15]

After the death of the controversial nun, her name receded into the Mexican annals for 300 years and did not resurface until the early twentieth century, thanks to Dorothy Schons. Did her male colleagues at the University of Texas not know Sor Juana? Did they devalue Schons's research on that Mexican nun due to some departmental bylaw or policy that dictated female professors could not research or publish on female writers? Did the *hombres necios* of the Romance Languages department vote against her getting tenure, despite the many years of service Schons had given to that department, and despite the published evidence of her knowledge and accomplishments that would have merited her promotion? Schmidhuber de la Mora is certain that Dorothy Schons conceived of Sor Juana's life as intractably linked—*"entrañablemente eslabonada"* (73)—to her own personal biography. In writing about Sor Juana, particularly in the more subjective (and subjunctive) voice of her unpublished novel, Dorothy Schons was writing about her own life-and-death struggles within the patriarchal academy that exploited her labor, appropriated her knowledge and dismissed her as a woman scholar.

Although Dorothy Schons was the first woman in Texas to earn a PhD, and the first female doctor of Romance languages in the United States, her research and publications on Sor Juana, an obscure Mexican nun at the time, did not count as true or tenurable scholarship. My educated guess as to what accounted for the patent disregard her department and university showed her was a three-fold institutional bias: against Mexico, against a woman scholar and against women studying other women—all of which ultimately got her fired from her job. Her academic appointment was terminated in 1960 for failure to achieve tenure. Is it any surprise that, alone and grieving for her dead sister, unknown and unappreciated as a scholar and unfairly dismissed from the career to which she had dedicated four decades of her life, she killed herself with a .32-caliber pistol on May 1, 1961, at the age of 69?[16] Or did she?

Prior to his critical biography on Dorothy Schons, Schmidhuber de la Mora wrote *La secreta amistad de Juana y Dorotea*, a five-act play that imagines what might have led to Schons's tragic and violent end. By juxtaposing Dorothy's and Juana's encounters with their respective *hombres necios*, Schmidhuber de la

Mora presents a plausible scenario of the excesses of patriarchal bias against women scholars, which did not end in Sor Juana's century. When Dorothy the character presents Dr. Herzberg, the chair of her department, with a syllabus for a seminar on Sor Juana Inés de la Cruz that she has been working on for over a year, he returns it to her dismissively, saying, *"No existe mujer en la literatura moderna que merezca un curso universitario."*[17] Not only does a woman not deserve a university course be taught in her name, but the fact that Sor Juana is from Mexico, *"un país sin literatura"* (de la Mora, *Secreta amistad,* 20), further dooms Dorothy's hopes of offering the course. Herzberg encourages her to stick to real writers, that is, male writers from Spain like Miguel de Cervantes and Calderón de la Barca, as those are the only writers who should be studied and taught in a department of Spanish literature.

In a later scene, Dorothy's colleague Dr. García warns her that her academic review is coming up and that her publications on that Mexican nun have put her tenure at risk. He would be willing to vote in her favor, he says, if she would agree to change the focus of her scholarship. *"En la historia de las universidades del mundo moderno no existe el caso de una mujer que estudie y enseñe a otra mujer"* (de la Mora, *Secreta amistad,* 22). To which Dorothy replies that if he only read Sor Juana he would discover her genius. Regretfully, he says, he has too much to read already, and since she won't change her mind, he must vote against her. It is in Act Five that Dorothy is given the pistol that will put her out of her existential misery.

In her comparison of the respective Sor Juana studies authored by Octavio Paz and Dorothy Schons, Georgina Sabat de Rivers asserts that not only did Schons in the 1930s have the capacity to see in Sor Juana what critics at the end of the twentieth century seem to be barely "discovering" about her, but also that Schons's

express intention was to center her interpretation on
the personality of the woman Sor Juana had been, and to
explain her reactions within this context. . . . As a woman,
Schons could not admit that Sor Juana [at the end of her
life] felt terrified and submitted to her fears, as Paz suggests, because that would have given the feminine sex a
fundamental weakness that was unacceptable (Sabat-
Rivers, 1985, 936-937, author's translation).

Having been trained by Schons, Sabat de Rivers was no doubt
speaking from an empirical perspective that her former professor
and mentor not only saw herself in Sor Juana, but also contextu-
alized Sor Juana's life and work within the feminist struggle
against the patriarchal oppression of women.

Decolonizing the Other Juana

Schons's story of Sor Juana's resistance to her oppressive
"environment," and her use of Sor Juana's story as a palimpsest
of how a great indigenous civilization was conquered by the
Spanish colonizers who wrought spiritual mayhem, biological
warfare through disease and violence and a genocidal imperative
against the native peoples that populated the "New World" shows
an early awareness of a gendered and racialized consciousness
decades before such a consciousness came into its own. Today
we call this consciousness decolonial feminism, a feminist praxis
that, as Chicana historian Emma Pérez explains, decolonizes the
Other (Sor Juana) as the speaking subject rather than seeing her
as the object who must be "spoken about [and] spoken for . . .
who cannot know what is good for [her], who cannot know how
to authorize [her] own narrative."[18]

To decolonize Sor Juana's "otherness," we must first locate
the speaking subject's different and often contradictory sites of
identity, the intersectionality of gender and race, ethnicity and
language, sexuality and social location, that constitute the speak-

ing subject's voice and story. Rather than trying to discern in Sor
Juana's oeuvre those literary elements that evoke or derive from
some canonical male writer, those "Gongoresque" or "Calderon-
ian" influences that Octavio Paz is so obsessed with in her work,
going so far as to say that Sor Juana, for all her unique "pecu-
liarities," was part of a tradition that included the Holy Bible, the
Church Fathers, as well as Góngora and Calderón. We may see
her as exceptional in her time, says Paz, but we must position her
work within the context of her male contemporaries, which Sor
Juana was compelled to imitate or rival.[19] There he goes again,
positioning Sor Juana's ideas in relation to the established scholarship of the day rather than attributing them to Sor Juana's own
genio y conocimiento, or genius and knowledge. Why not, as we
say in Spanish, *darle la palabra*? Because in giving Sor Juana
the word, Paz would be forced to recognize her as the speaking
subject, and that would grant her agency, and that would mean
she, as a woman, was bestowing upon herself the authority to
write, read and publish whatever she wanted, and that as a nun,
she was breaking her vows of obedience, poverty, humility and
enclosure. Sor Juana's celebrity during her lifetime was outside
the norm, and therefore Other; but insomuch as her illuminated
mind was constructed as a manifestation of her "masculinity,"
then she could be admired, envied, recognized on the one hand,
and punished, censured and silenced, on the other.

I disagree with Ilan Stavans' assessment of Sor Juana as "an
impersonator of masculinity" who "had to revamp, even reinvent,
her feminine side" (Sayers Peden, 1997, xvi). Seeing her as an
impersonator assumes that only masculinity was entitled to a life
of the mind and reduces Sor Juana's lifelong quest for knowledge
to mimicry and pretense. Of her supposed feminine side, Sor
Juana tells us in her poem, "In Reply to a Gentleman from Peru
Who Sent Her Clay Vessels While Suggesting She Would Better
Be a Man," that, she entered the convent

so that, *if* I am female,
none substantiate that state.
    I know, too, that they were wont
to call wife, or woman, in the Latin
uxor, only those who wed,
though wife or woman might be virgin.
    So in my case, it is not seemly
that I be viewed as feminine,
as I will never be a woman
who may as woman serve a man.
    I know only that my body,
not to either state inclined,
is neuter, abstract, guardian
of only what my Soul consigns. (Sayers Peden, 1997, 141)

If she is neither masculine nor feminine, neither male nor female, neither wife nor woman, what is she? And what did she
mean by calling her body "neuter" and "abstract"? True, a nun
was expected to neuter her sex with her vow of chastity, and to
make her body an abstraction under the black veil and habit, nothing more than a vessel in which to guard her Soul. Somehow,
though, I think she's using Church dogma to subvert the binary
gender codes that would prevent her from learning and force her
to a reductive biological destiny. In other words, Sor Juana enters
the convent and becomes a nun so that she can cease being a
woman and instead inhabit a gender-neutral state.

    It is no wonder that Sor Juana was such an anomaly in seven-
teenth-century New Spain. From the intriguing "*marisabia*" or girl
scholar of her youth who was invited to serve as a lady-in-waiting
at the viceregal court, to the irregular "bride of Christ" who joined
the convent to fulfill her scholarly vocation, ignoring all the pro-
tocols of her cloistered position, to the scandalous "*la peor de
todas,*" or worst of all women and all nuns, who was almost ex-

communicated by the Holy Inquisition. Sor Juana was indeed a rare bird. As Georgina Sabat de Rivers concludes, "[n]uestra Sor Juana del siglo XVII fue esa mujer revolucionaria para cuya existencia se pueden hallar resquicios en la crítica feminista de hoy."[20]

Like Sor Juana, Dorothy Schons was also a revolutionary woman. They were both solitary, brilliant minds with a talent for research and writing who saw too clearly the oppression of their sex by *hombres necios* who resented their intelligence, their influence and their accomplishments; *hombres necios* who went out of their way to orchestrate the conditions that eventuated in the women's demise. We decolonize women like Dorothy and Sor Juana by listening to their stories, by scrutinizing the sexual politics, the power dynamics, the struggles, the victories and the defeats each had to contend with in her day and by locating them within the sisterhood of revolutionary women.

In the "Apologia" to her novel, Dorothy Schons explains that she wrote a fictive treatment of the life of this most illustrious Mexican nun because there was little scholarship available on a figure who had seemingly passed into critical oblivion 300 years after the apex of her fame and glory. Nor did she find any secondary sources that would substantiate her standpoint epistemology of Sor Juana as the first feminist of the Americas. The personal details and ruminations of "A Chronicle of Old Mexico," then, can only come from two places: Sor Juana herself, and Schons's own "decolonial imaginary." By extrapolating the personal details Sor Juana left us in her own poetry and epistolary work, by paralleling Sor Juana's struggle against the Church patriarchs of the seventeenth century with her own stubborn positionality as an anomalous Golden Age scholar whom her male colleagues were trying desperately to discredit, Schons's novel portrayed the *proto-feminist* behind this enlightened, albeit (in Schons' view) penitent mind.

Rebel with a Cause

Sor Juana is a primordial example of the "bad woman" stereotype that I wrote about in *[Un]Framing the "Bad Woman,"* the woman who disobeys, who does not follow protocol, who resists patriarchal inscriptions of her sex and gender, who flaunts her attributes and who persists in her rebellious ways against all forms of censure and punishment. "World, why do you insist/ on persecuting me?" Sor Juana asks in Poem 146: "How do I offend, when all I seek/ is to put beauty in my mind,/ and not my mind on beauty?/ I value not treasures or riches;/ and thus, it gives me more pleasure/ to put riches in my thoughts/ and not my thoughts on riches."[21] For Sor Juana, beauty and enrichment meant the cultivation of the mind and the spirit through poetry, music, art and especially writing, learning and producing knowledge. The superficial notions of beauty did not interest her, for these included not just aesthetic concerns, but also the qualities that a society ruled by men had deemed "beautiful," and therefore desirable, in women: purity, modesty, humility, maternity, passivity, to which had to be added the poverty, chastity and docility demanded of nuns in the Church if they expected redemption from their sins. Because she defied every one of those traditional norms of both a "good woman" and a "good bride of Christ," because she "refused to comply with those social [expectations] by which 'good girls' and 'good women' were constructed" (Gaspar de Alba, *Unframing*, 19) she did everything in her power to resist her erasure from history, and she persisted in her lifelong quest for equality and emancipation. Thus, the wealth that she accumulated was not financial wealth, per se (although she did make capital investments in the convent's real estate possessions and left a dowry for her niece, Belilla, who had joined the Order of Saint Jerome), but rather the rich legacy of knowledge she created with the indefatigable labors of her mind and body.

As Margaret Sayers Peden affirms in her Translator's Note to *Poems, Protest, and a Dream: Selected Writings of Sor Juana Inés de la Cruz*, Sor Juana's work not only challenged "the wrath of male establishment," but also asserted "her right as a woman to explore the very foundations of knowledge, the world of the intellect, the sphere from which a mere nun should have been excluded" (viii).

Sor Juana left a legacy of decolonial feminist thought three hundred years before the feminist revolution. She also left several inklings of her lesbian desire and her persecuted soul within patriarchy in her plays, poetry and prose. By focusing on Sor Juana's own words and primary sources (walking in her shoes), by listening to the silences that she purposefully inserted into her texts (in-habiting her life), by filtering her unwittingly closeted story through the intersectional parameters of my own Chicana lesbian writer/academic/poet's subjectivity, my novel and my critical essays on Sor Juana exercise a decolonial feminist revision of Latin America's Tenth Muse. As I wrote elsewhere, "This rewriting of [Sor Juana's] colonial narrative from a Chicana lesbian female symbolic is how I track Sor Juana's agency across the colonial landscape of both New Spain and the *sorjuanista* imaginary" (Gaspar de Alba, *Unframing* 19).

In my Chicana lesbian feminist reframing of Sor Juana, I track the poetic clues that she left us in her primary texts—such as the lines quoted above from her response to that Peruvian who was questioning her gender; or the poem in which she eats the secret note sent to her by "the palace," i.e., code for *la Condesa*; or another in which she pleads her beloved's forgiveness for her silence, for not being able to say everything there is to say about her feelings and her desires[22]—to locate Sor Juana's "*sitio y lengua*," a theory invented by Emma Pérez in 1990 that situates identity in social, cultural, historical and linguistic locations, and desire in the lesbian tongue.[23]

It is not by accident or serendipity that La Condesa de Paredes referred to Sor Juana by the honorific that Plato bestowed on the great lesbian poet, Sappho—the Tenth Muse, or "*décima musa*"—in the long title she, as editor, gave to her beloved's first volume of collected works.[24] In that volume, the poems Sor Juana writes to her "*divina* Lysis," her nickname for *la Condesa*, like the requiems she wrote to the previous vicereine, Marquesa de Mancera, known as Laura in the poems, who took the teenaged Juana under her wing when she lived at court, have a completely different tone and speaking subject than the sacred panegyrics commissioned by the Church council or the tributes she was hired to write by the nobles and other aristocrats who often visited her in the convent's *locutorio* (sitting room) or her more ludic pieces that showed the virtuosity of her wordplay. Her poems to Lysis and Laura are the real love poems of Sor Juana, and they reveal to those of us who can, in Sor Juana's words, "hear [her] with [our] eyes"[25] what kind of Sister she really was, a sister who loved and was loved by another woman, her mind and her flesh.[26]

In 1999, the University of New Mexico press published *Sor Juana's Second Dream*, my radical Chicana lesbian feminist interpretation of Sor Juana's life and work, written in both first and third person, and composed of her own words and invented pages of her Sapphic diary and secret letters that together signify the possibility of a Second Dream. In opposition to Sor Juana's *First Dream*, in which the Queen of Night (the Moon) loses her daily battle with the Light of Male Reason (the Sun), I wanted to imagine what our Tenth Muse's life might have been like had she actually done more than dream about giving free rein to the Dark Queen of her nightly journeys into the body. What if, I mused, the outcome of her *First Dream* had been different, if passion rather than reason had won the battle between the Sun and the Moon? What would our Mexicana and Chicana feminist lives be like today if Sor Juana's *conocimiento* (and the accumulated knowledge of all the women mystics, scholars, philosophers and poets who preceded and followed her) had inspired, rather than threatened, the enlightened minds of her/their/our generation? Perhaps this is the Third Dream.

If there is such a thing as poetic justice, the fact that my archives are also in the Benson Collection at UT Austin, along with those of other contemporary Chicana feminist theorists, poets and scholars, might provide some solace to the solitary soul of Dorothy Schons. Perhaps Dorothy's spirit will tiptoe into the Alicia Gaspar de Alba Papers, find those eight boxes of first drafts of what became *Sor Juana's Second Dream* and turn those archived pages with her ghostly fingers, reading with abandon those graphic scenes of Sor Juana's auto-erotic moments and her lovemaking with *la Condesa* that I had to leave on the cutting-room floor when revising the manuscript for publication. Perhaps these sexual and quixotic scenes will shed a different light on the tortured and penitent Sor Juana that Schons penned in "A Chronicle of Old Mexico" and help her revendicate Sor Juana as a predecessor of both the feminist cause and lesbian identity politics in the New World.

6
THE PIÑATA DREAM

I.

X. Mary Espinosa

She wrote her name at the top of the page but wasn't sure if she should write in her whole name–Xochitl Maria Espinosa—or just the name she had gone by since she was in third grade, Mary Espinosa. She used the X only for her writing. Her biggest fantasy was seeing "X. Mary Espinosa" on the cover of her first novel.

What is your earliest remembered dream and your earliest memory, and what do you think they say about who you are today? Please write a paragraph for each part of the question.

"I've never thought about my earliest remembered dream. + think this is like asking + ~~believe this may not be the first thing~~

"Shit!" She crumpled the paper and turned up the volume on her Walkman, keeping time with her pencil. The Alan Parsons Project was singing about confusion, a feeling swirling around in her own blood at this moment. She had come to the cemetery, one of her favorite places in Iowa City, to write the essay on the questionnaire, believing that the quiet graveyard in the hazy autumn morning would be just the place for her to remember her earliest dream.

Instead, she found herself thinking about her poetry class, about the poems they had workshopped so far that she could never have written. It wasn't because she didn't understand the assignments or because she was a teenager and didn't know anything about life, as the professor had insinuated, but because she was a fiction writer, a storyteller, and she wrote story-poems. Hadn't they ever heard of narrative poetry and prose poetry? Oh, but the class didn't go for that. The professor was hung up on enjambment and didn't believe in prepositions. Even imagery was something less than allegory. Imagery, they said, was just concrete objects in words. A wheelbarrow didn't have to be symbolic of the womb of life and the story of creation. It was just a wheelbarrow, they insisted, a thing to carry dirt in and to catch the rain, as if the dirt and the rain weren't characters in the same plot.

The class was starting to plug her up, in every sense. And when anybody reminded her that she was the only seventeen-year-old ever to get a scholarship to the Iowa Writers' Workshop, she'd pretend to put a finger down her throat and gag as a response. She was also the only one in the Workshop who had a book of stories published. Besides, she was female and had a Mexican last name. Even though there was a town full of Mexicans fourteen miles away from Iowa City, even though there was a Chicano House on campus, Mexican Americans weren't exactly a constituency in the writers' community. She opened her thermos, poured herself the dregs of her chamomile tea and smoothed out the crumpled paper. Why couldn't she write this essay? She finally had the chance to string sentences together, but her memory was acting weird, shy almost. Right now, the only dream she remembered was the piñata dream, and only because it came as regularly as her period. She looked up at the nine-foot black angel that graced the tomb on which she always leaned and waited for the angel's eyes to slide down from her black forehead as they always did when she was underneath.

"I'll make a deal with you, Rodina," she said out loud when the angel's eyes appeared. "If you help me remember, I'll come visit you every day, even in winter. If I don't write this essay, I can't go to the appointment. What do you say, Rodina?"

She had named the angel after the woman whose tomb the giant statue guarded: Rodina Feldevertova. Another immigrant to the Midwest, just like X. Mary Espinosa. But Rodina's eyes rolled back into her head, and Mary knew that her only alternative now was to fake it. She took the clipping from *The Daily Iowan* out of her pocket and read it again to get her imagination pumping.

PANDORA'S JUNGLE
Where your dreams meet the Tarot
Hazel Eaves, L.I.C.S.W.
The alternative to counseling. For Womyn only.
Learn how to release your own ills and blessings.
Call for appointment or information. 362-7155.

Mary had called on Saturday, had gone over to meet this Hazel Eaves and to get the questionnaire that she had to fill out before their first session. The last thing on the questionnaire was this essay that she couldn't write and that Hazel Eaves had told her was imperative as the foundation for the reading.

She looked out over the graveyard and felt lost. Sure, she could write a weird dream, a bizarre scene for a memory, but if the interpretation of the piñata dream depended on this essay, and this essay was only fiction, the interpretation wasn't going to work, and Mary would never know why the piñata dream had been haunting her for so long. How could she fake something as important as this? In her ears, Chuck Mangione was doing "Feels So Good." She took the headphones off, screwed the plastic cup back onto the thermos, and stuffed the Walkman and the thermos into her backpack. She touched the hem of the black angel's dress before leaving the tomb, then walked her bike to the asphalt path that led out of the cemetery. Hazel Eaves would just have to understand that after a month and a half of reading poetry and trying to exorcise the prose out of her poems, Mary couldn't write an essay. They'd just have to do something else for a foundation.

II.

"Am I late? Your roommate said you were back here."

The husky voice startled Hazel out of her meditation. She sat up on her mat and looped the wires of her glasses behind her ears. The girl was wearing bright yellow bicycling tights, purple high-tops and a black baseball cap with a red pitchfork as a logo.

"Not really," Hazel said. "I was planning to sit out here anyway. This'll be the last of our late summer, I'm afraid." She reached an arm out to the girl. "Help an old lady up," she said, and the girl held her elbow out for support. "Let's go to the picnic table. Are you ready to explore Pandora's Jungle?"

"That's my unconscious, right?"

"Right," said Hazel. "I like your cap. What's the pitchfork about?"

"El Paso Diablos," the girl answered as she slipped onto the bench across the table from Hazel. "The dust-devils of Dudley Field."

"A piece of home, I gather," said Hazel. "Why were you late? Having second thoughts?"

The girl ran her fingers over the carved teakwood box that held Hazel's materials for the session. Hazel noticed that her nails were even closer to extinction than they had been on Saturday.

"I was in the cemetery trying to write that essay for the application," the girl said, "but I didn't get very far."

"Let me see," said Hazel.

The girl unzipped her pack and pulled out the questionnaire Hazel glanced down at the first page. Sagittarius. Only child. Catholic. First time away from home.

"Why were you in the cemetery?" Hazel asked, flipping to the back of the questionnaire.

"I go there sometimes," the girl said.

"I don't see the essay."

The girl took a wrinkled sheet out and handed it to Hazel.

"I see," said Hazel.

The girl started nibbling at what was left of her thumbnail. "Can we still do it?" she asked.

"Are you having a hard time remembering?" asked Hazel. "Pandora can be a bit stubborn at times."

"I don't know," said the girl. "I attributed it to writer's block."

"Well, maybe you should tell me what happened in West Liberty again. We can try to use that as a springboard for the reading."

"On the afternoon of September 13th," the girl recounted, and Hazel could tell the girl had been watching one too many *Law & Order* episodes, "I saw a flyer in Memorial Union announcing a *Día de Independencia* fiesta in West Liberty on Sunday the 15th. I thought it would be interesting to see how Midwestern Mexican Americans celebrate Mexican Independence Day, so I rode my bike out there and found out. I was more than a little surprised to see Old Glory hanging next to the Mexican flag there in the 4-H Club, and when they opened the festivities with the 'The Star-Spangled Banner' instead of the Mexican national anthem (which they played after 'The Star-Spangled Banner'), I knew it wasn't the kind of *Independencia* fiesta that the people of Juárez would've understood."

"And what did you see at this fiesta that reminded you of your dream?" Hazel asked, trying to steer the girl back on track.

"A piñata," said the girl, "an old-fashioned, star-shaped piñata almost exactly like the one in my dream."

"Explain 'star-shaped piñata,'" said Hazel. "I'm not up-to-date on Mexican culture."

"Neither am I," said the girl, "but I do know that they don't make star-shaped piñatas anymore, at least not in Juárez. The ones they sell at the mercado look like burros and Superman, but my grandpa told me that when he was a kid, and even when my mom was a kid, the piñatas in those days were stars: round in the middle with papier-mâché cones sticking out and crepe paper tassels hanging off the tips of the cones."

The girl unclipped her fountain pen from her blouse and scratched out a drawing of the piñata on the wrinkled essay sheet.

"The round part was actually a clay pot covered up with colored crepe paper," the girl's exegesis continued, "and this is where the candy was, as well as fruits and nuts and little toys. You see, piñatas used to be only for Christmas—that's what my grandpa told me—and that's why they were so beautiful and so special, and they were shaped like stars to symbolize the Star of Bethlehem. Now they use piñatas mainly for birthdays and also for some special holidays, but I've never seen a star-shaped piñata except for in my dream. And then to see one in West Liberty, Iowa, of all places! Talk about authentic freak-out!"

"You said this piñata in West Liberty was 'almost exactly' like the one in your dream," Hazel reminded her. "What was the difference?"

"Why don't I just tell you the dream?" the girl said. "You do want to hear the story of the dream, don't you?"

"Of course," said Hazel. "Let me get myself set up." She opened the teakwood box and took out a tiny tape recorder. "Ready," she said, pressing the REC button.

The girl had a suspicious look in her eye. "You didn't say anything about taping the session."

"Since we've agreed that you're going to let me use your dream in the book I'm writing," said Hazel, "that's what the waiver you signed was all about. . . ."

"I thought you meant your interpretation of it," the girl put in, "not the whole dream, word for word. It's like it won't belong to me anymore, just because I don't have to pay you for this reading."

Hazel pulled her glasses off and rubbed her eyes. "Look, you can back out of the agreement if it makes you feel better," she said. "I didn't realize you wanted to copyright your dream."

"I'm a writer," said the girl. "I just might do that."

Hazel hooked her glasses back on. "Fine," she said. "When we're done, I'll give you the tape. But it's important to have the dream on tape in case you make any allusions or drop any clues or have any flashes of insight as you're telling it to me. Those nuances and innuendoes of the moment might hold the seeds of the real meaning. Shall we proceed?"

"Okay, I'm about eight or nine in this dream," the girl began suddenly, "and my mom is dressing me up to go to a birthday party across the border in Juárez. I've got this white dress on, real shiny material, like satin, with a huge blue satin bow at the back of my waist and another one on my head. I'm also wearing white gloves and white patent leather shoes; it feels like I'm going to a Holy Communion instead of a birthday party. I'm not too thrilled about going to this party. It's not just my clothes that make me uncomfortable; it's something else that I never remember at this point in the dream. But my mom is making me go, kind of dragging me there, actually.

"We have to go across the bridge, as I said, because this party is in Juárez, but it's not happening at anybody's house. The piñata is right there on the levee of the Rio Grande. I can see the piñata hanging between two trees as we come over the bridge and look down past the Tortilla Curtain.

"Anyway, we go through the turnstile and then go around the corner at the Mexican customs building and head towards the *colonias*, the poorest section of Juárez, which is directly across the river from the university. As we're walking along the riverbank, I can hear all the kids at the party screaming and laughing, rattling on in Spanish, and I begin to realize in the dream that this is part of what makes me uncomfortable about going to this party. Everybody's speaking Spanish, and I can't speak Spanish very well. (This is not just part of the dream. I really do have a gringa accent from having gone to school on the El Paso side most of my life and not being allowed to speak Spanish at any of those schools.) So I decide not to talk or play with anybody at this party. I feel real stupid in this fancy dress, too, because all the other kids look like the little beggars that hang out on the Córdoba bridge.

"As soon as we get to where the piñata's hanging, all the kids get in line to take their turns at breaking it. It's the most incredible piñata I've ever seen, a giant star made of translucent pink glass that catches the sun and reflects it into rainbows on the dirt of the levee; even the tassels are made of glass, strings of glass beads that sound like little bells in the wind. I don't want to get in line. Not only am I boycotting the party, I also can't believe they want to shatter that glass star. It seems holy to me, but not holy in a peaceful way like the Virgin Mary, holy in a scary way, like when a *penitente* whips himself in a Holy Week procession.

"I tell my mom I don't want to stay at this party. That I'm scared and want to go home, but she tells me I have to get in line and take my turn like all the other kids, that it's rude if we leave before the piñata has been broken. She pulls a handkerchief out of her pocket and blindfolds me. I try to pull away from her. I tell her I'm at the end of the line, so how come she's putting a blindfold on me if it's not even my turn yet? She tells me everybody's got to wear a blindfold. Nobody can see this piñata being broken, she says, because the glass might get into your eyes and blind you.

"She leaves me standing there, with the blindfold so tight I can feel the knot digging into the back of my head. I call out to her not to leave me alone, that I'm scared because I know I'm gonna get punished if I break this piñata, but she tells me over and over: *No tengas miedo*, Xochitl. Don't be afraid, Xochitl. (My first name is Xochitl, which is an Aztec name, but my mom told me that the priest wouldn't baptize me unless I had a Christian name to go along with it, so they named me Xochitl María, and the nuns started calling me Mary in the fourth grade.)

"Anyway, the line is moving quickly. Nobody's even hit a cone on the piñata. You only get three swings when it's your turn, and if you don't hit anything in those three swings, then you pass the stick to the next kid and the next kid, until finally somebody breaks it and all the candy falls out. That's when everybody goes wild.

"All of a sudden, a pair of hands starts turning me around to make me dizzy, so I know it's my turn to swing at the piñata. I keep seeing the image of that glass star in my head, that holy symbol of something I don't understand. I call out to my mom again, but she keeps telling me not to be afraid, that she promises I won't get punished. Then the stick is in my hands, and I'm so scared I start pissing my pants; I can feel it running down the inside of my legs and into my socks. The other kids are chanting *¡Quiébrala! ¡Quiébrala!* Break it! Break it!

"And then all these hands are at my back, pushing me closer and closer to the piñata, and I turn around to threaten them with my stick, yelling 'I want to go home! Let me go home!' I swing the stick back to hit those hands that are pushing me, and then I hear the shattering behind me. I've killed the glass piñata. And I know it's some kind of sin.

"I always wake up terrified. I don't know why I keep having this dream, but I tell you, seeing that star-shaped piñata in West Liberty scared me so much I cried.

"The funny thing is, though, that my mom hated Mexico. We were from there, from the interior, but she hated talking about it, and she never wanted to go across the bridge to the mercado or the bullfights with my dad and me. She used to say there was too much pain in Mexico, and that she couldn't stand remembering the pain. She never would've taken me to a party in the *colonias*."

The girl took a deep breath and sighed as she exhaled. She took off her cap and tousled her short hair. Hazel clicked off the tape recorder.

"When did you lose your mother?" asked Hazel.

The girl looked Hazel straight in the eye. "My mom killed herself four years ago," she said in a cold voice. "She shot up too much insulin and gave herself a heart attack."

Hazel raised her eyebrows but didn't say anything. She opened the box again and took out the silk-wrapped Morgan-Greer deck. "What I want you to do now," she said, unwrapping the deck slowly, "is to go through the tarot and choose five cards that will represent the five most important images in your dream. Then spread them out on the table, following the sequence the images had in the dream. Understand?"

She set the deck face down in front of the girl, and the girl nodded.

"I'll be back in fifteen minutes," Hazel said. "I know what it feels like to lose a parent at that age."

The girl nodded again, but she was staring at the stars on the back of the top card. Hazel left her alone and went to brew a fresh pot of coffee. On the way in, she noticed the sky had a violet tint to it. The autumn rains were coming.

"We may have to come inside. Looks like a storm," she called to the girl.

The girl did not answer. She was wiping her eyes with the sleeve of her blouse and continued to sit at the picnic table.

Hazel opened the screen door that led to her kitchen. She needed to write down her first thoughts on this piñata dream. What an archetype!

III.

The memory had slipped down from Mary's forehead like the eyes of the black angel:

"Come help Mami, Xochitl. The tea's almost ready." Her mom never called her Mary or María.

The pungent odor of the boiling herbs hung like tar in the kitchen, the vapor clinging to Mary's skin.

"Get the honey," her mom would say, and Mary would dig the measuring spoon into the honey and draw out two tablespoons for the tea that her mom was straining into a clay cup. It was Mary's job to stir the tea until all the honey dissolved. Her mom got the needle ready. Mary held her breath as her mom sat on the chair, lifted her skirt, rolled down her stockings and shot the insulin into both thighs.

"I'm going to lie down on your bed, Xochitl. Don't forget to bring me the tea in fifteen minutes to help Mami come out of her trance." Always the same words.

Mary would wait just outside the bedroom door, eyes glued to the second hand of her watch, afraid of thinking, terrified her dad would come home early or her grandpa would stop by with a bag of groceries. Only she and her mom could know about this secret ritual. If anybody else found out that her mom was putting herself into trances to speak to the Virgin face to face, the Virgin would punish her mom and take her life away. So Mary guarded the secret as carefully as she counted the 900 seconds.

Mary tried to make the memory roll back into her head so that she could concentrate on finding the five cards. She turned the deck over and looked at the first card. A naked man and woman standing in a garden like Adam and Eve. Not that one. She turned to the next card. A skeleton in a black-hooded cape holding a scythe. She set that card on the table. Three more cards and then she came upon one with a big, orange sun that reminded her of the piñata. She laid that card beside the other one. Eight more cards and she found one with a blindfolded woman. This one for sure. The next card made her set the whole deck down. The devil was staring at her through a goat's head. She went to the next card, and the next, and the next, then looked back at the devil card, then moved forward again, counting.

She passed twenty-five cards. The twenty-sixth one showed five hands holding five sticks. All the hands pushing her to hit the piñata, she thought, placing the card beside the blindfolded woman.

She needed one more card, but she couldn't figure out which important image she had left out. She looked at the four cards on the table and realized that the missing image was the border. She combed through the rest of the deck and found only one card that could, with some imagination, represent the border. It had eight branches slanted over the top and at the bottom, a blue river separating two pieces of green land.

She started ordering the cards but felt raindrops pattering on the back of her neck, then heard the squeaky hinges of the screen door.

"I knew it!" called Hazel, running across the lawn. "We better . . . These autumn storms." The rest of her sentence dispersed in the rising wind.

Hazel tossed the tape recorder and the tarot deck into a bag. Mary shielded the five cards with her backpack as she followed Hazel into the house. The sky was a purple bruise, and the wind whipped the yellow branches of the weeping willow in the yard.

Mary shuddered as another memory echoed in her head. Don't go to the levee, Xochitl. La Llorona hides in the weeping willows on the levee. She's a kidnapper.

"Just made it!" said Hazel as the downpour drenched the boards of the back stoop. "Have a seat. Coffee's ready." She pointed to the bay window where the table and chairs were nearly buried in a jungle of African violets.

The rain sluiced off the windowpanes. Mary pulled a chair out, and a tabby cat peered up at her through emerald eyes.

"That's Athena," said Hazel, setting two mugs on the table. "Move over, Athena."

The cat uncurled itself and sprang off the chair. Mary slipped into the warm seat.

"Any luck with the cards?" asked Hazel, pouring the coffee from a percolator.

"I just have to put them in order."

Hazel dragged her chair to sit beside her. Mary held the cards like a poker hand and moved them in and out of different slots until she had the right order.

"This is easier than I thought," she said. "Like putting a story into pictures." She laid the cards before Hazel one by one. "Here's the setting," she explained, "but you have to pretend the river and the land are brown instead of green and blue like that. El Paso's in the desert."

"Which side is El Paso in this card?" asked Hazel.

"The one with the castle," said Mary without any doubt. The castle was her house in Sunset Heights.

"I thought so," said Hazel. She held her mug under her nose and inhaled the steam of the coffee.

"The piñata's the conflict," said Mary. "Here's the main character. All these hands are the obstacles. And this is the denouement. See what I mean? It's a perfect story."

Hazel sipped on her coffee as she studied the cards. "The tarot makes things so clear."

"Interpret," said Mary.

"I'm going to talk about the meaning of the spread first," Hazel told her. "Then we'll associate the story of the spread with the story of your dream. Okay?"

"I'm ready." Mary could feel her pulse beating in her neck.

"The opening card tells us what the issue is," Hazel began, "and you've opened with the Eight of Rods. Rods are the suit that

represents the Self, particularly the Self-concept, the identity."
She took another sip from her mug.

Mary tasted the coffee, found it too bitter and pushed the mug
aside.

"The Eight of Rods tells us that you are in the process of re-
grouping your Self-concept. You're analyzing your identity, trying to determine who you are."

"Everybody's doing that," said Mary.

"True," said Hazel, "in some form or another, we are all engaged in that process, but remember, you picked this card, and
you chose to open the spread with it. This means your process,
your awareness of the process, is probably your first priority right
now, though you may not realize it. You also may not realize you
have a guide." She tapped the Sun card. "This is your guide, your
beacon, the star that you should follow. The Sun is a universal
symbol of life, but in the tarot, it also implies an inner journey
that will enrich your life. It could be a spiritual journey, or a quest
for the Self, even a physical trip or vacation. What the Sun card
means is that you should embark on your journey, whatever it is;
it is a bright time to go."

Hazel poured herself another cup of coffee. The storm rattled
the windows.

"Any questions so far?" asked Hazel.

Mary shook her head, rubbing her hands to warm them.
Under the table, the cat grazed Mary's leg.

"Swords," Hazel continued, pointing to the card of the blindfolded woman, "represent the conscious mind, the conscious
awareness. Obviously, our main character here doesn't want to be
aware of something. The blindfold indicates that she doesn't want
to see, she doesn't want to be conscious of this questioning of
her identity. She's got two swords in her hands, which represent
two options she must choose between, and she could use these
swords to remove the blindfold. But, you see, removing the blindfold is the equivalent of making the choice, and she can only

make the choice if she's aware of the options, but she doesn't want to be responsible for that. So the blindfold stays."

"I should be making an outline of this," said Mary, reaching down to take a notebook out of her pack.

"Now we move on to the Five of Rods," said Hazel, "another identity card. This one tells us that you are already experiencing changes inside yourself, even though you aren't aware of the causes. Changes, of course, bring conflicts; that's why all the hands look like they're engaged in a brawl. You could say that each rod in each hand represents a different aspect of your identity, aspects that are not very compatible right now, and that are manifesting themselves in a kind of chaos."

Mary scribbled "identity chaos" in her notebook.

Hazel twirled her mug between her hands before going on to the Death card. Athena rubbed against Mary's leg again.

"Your cat's making me nervous," Mary said.

"Athena, get out of here!" said Hazel, but Athena curled herself under the table and kept her green gaze on Mary's ankles.

"The good thing about chaos," Hazel continued, "is that it always leads to catharsis. The denouement, as you called the Death card, is a very positive card here, but you probably chose it for its negative connotations, right? Probably to symbolize how afraid you were at having 'killed the glass piñata,' as you put it."

"What's positive about death?"

"The Death card doesn't mean physical death," explained Hazel, "especially not in this context. The Death card simply means an end to something. This spread has shown us that the something involves your identity, your quest for self-definition, a journey that's creating havoc right now, mainly because you can't see what your options are. The Death card tells us that the chaos will end if you choose to remove the blindfold. The outcome of the journey will be the death of confusion, which means the birth of clarity. You see, the Death card is really an indicator of rebirth. The scythe in the skeleton's hand is a harvest tool, and the crop to be harvested is the inner self."

Mary picked up her mug and swallowed some of the cold, bitter coffee. "This is what my dream means?" she asked.

"Associatively speaking, yes," said Hazel. "Let me just ask you a couple of questions before I give you the punchline. First, exactly when did you start having this dream?"

"I don't remember . . . a long time ago."

"How long? What grade were you in? Was your mother still alive?"

Mary's mouth opened. She looked at Hazel, then down at the cards, then back at Hazel. "No," she said. "It started the same day my mom died. We were riding in my grandpa's car back from the funeral, and I fell asleep against his arm and had that dream."

"That would explain the birthday party," said Hazel. "Pandora often gives us images that seem opposite to each other. The other side of death is birth; the other side of a funeral would be a birthday party."

"But it wasn't my mom's birthday," said Mary.

"Maybe it was your birthday," Hazel suggested. "Maybe that's why you're all dressed up and why you're the one who has to break the piñata. After the funeral, you probably felt that a part of you had died, and indeed it had, but that death signified the birth of something else. The birth of a new identity, perhaps."

"What new identity?"

Hazel crossed her legs into a lotus position on the chair. "Wait," she said, "tell me about the flowers."

Mary felt ice cubes sliding down her back. "What flowers? The funeral flowers?"

"These flowers," said Hazel. "All the sunflowers on the Sun card and the white rose on the Death card. What do they have to do with your dream?"

"I didn't even pay any attention to those," said Mary. "I was going for the major images in the cards."

"You may not have been paying attention," Hazel smiled, "but Pandora was. These flowers, for example, symbolize fertility, the fertility given by the sun, the ripening of your conscious mind, the seeds of awareness. In other words, the sunflowers contain the seeds of your new identity. And the white rose here, is you, blooming on the Death card. Didn't you say you were dressed all in white in this dream?"

Mary stared at the pink and purple blooms of the African violets on the table, at the downy stems that were so different from the thorny stem of the white rose. "Oh my god," she gasped. "My last name, Espinosa, means full of thorns."

Hazel clenched her fist and looked up at the ceiling. "Thank you, Pandora," she said. "What does your other name mean? The Aztec one?"

"Xochitl? I don't know. I never asked."

Hazel uncrossed her legs. "Okay, here's my interpretation of your dream," she said, pausing slightly for a dramatic effect that brought Mary to the edge of her chair.

"You are at Xochitl's birthday party," Hazel began, "which is happening on the most impoverished side of your psychic border, the Mexican side of your identity. And you're dressed for a communion ceremony because, in effect, you are going to commune with Xochitl, the mysterious one, the part of you that you've repressed because she represents negative things like your mother's pain, or poverty, or not fitting in.

"But Xochitl lives inside the piñata. I'm interpreting the star-shaped piñata as a symbol for Mexico. And the piñata holds this mysterious identity of yours that you're afraid to see because of its negative connotations. But remember, the blindfolded woman has a choice to make: you can continue to see Xochitl in a negative light, or you can take the cover off her eyes and see her in the light of this glass piñata. Either way, you're going to break the piñata. That's Pandora's way of telling you that you need to confront this issue on a conscious level. And the Death card suggests that at the end of the process, you will experience a rebirth."

"You mean I, as Mary, am going to die, and I, as Xochitl, am going to be reborn?" Mary asked, frowning. "What do I have to do, change my name and move to Mexico?"

"I mean Xochitl and Mary will become one," said Hazel. "You don't have to go to any extremes for that to happen, but maybe you should find out who Xochitl is. What's her history? What's her genealogy? What does her name mean? Pandora already knows all this, but she won't release the information until you're ready to commune with Xochitl, and what better way than to communicate through the medium of your own writing? You told me on Saturday that writing is your truth. If you infuse that truth with Xochitl's spirit, I think you could achieve a true balance between the two sides of your identity. And that's when you would experience your rebirth."

Rebirth. Truth. Spirit. Balance.

Platitudes, that's what all this was. New Age bullshit platitudes!

"This is bullshit," she said to Hazel, although she could not understand why she had suddenly started to cry. Why suddenly all her bones ached, and her heart felt as though it had been ripped out by the root.

"What did you do to me?" said Mary, wiping her nose with the inside of her wrist.

Hazel put her hand on Mary's shoulder. "It's a lot to deal with, I know. This is the way these trips to Pandora's Jungle usually turn out the first time."

"I have to go," said Mary. She reached down for her backpack and found Athena sprawled on it. She laughed in spite of the tears, and then the crying got worse, and the tears just sluiced off Mary's face.

"Let me get you a tissue," said Hazel, but Mary picked up her pack and headed for the back door.

"Isn't your bike out front?" asked Hazel, and Mary realized she'd forgotten about her bike, which she'd left standing against the side of the house and was probably blowing down to the Iowa River by now.

Again, Mary laughed, a repressed hysterical kind of laughing that hurt her chest as she stumbled out of the kitchen and to the hallway where she found her bike. Hazel's roommate had probably brought it in. Mary lifted the stand with her heel and walked the ten-speed out the door. Outside, she could not distinguish between her tears and the rain that blurred her vision.

When she got home, her clothes were a second skin, and her teeth chattered so loudly it gave her a headache. She had not stopped crying. The only thing she wanted was to hide. She scribbled a note to her roommate, her cousin Ivon, to please not disturb her and to tell whoever called her on the phone that she was hiding and couldn't talk to anybody. Then, she took a hot shower and crawled into the flannel sheets. She cried the way she had not cried since her mom's funeral.

Late in the afternoon, she remembered her poetry class but knew there was no way she could go. She got up and put a tape on, then lay in bed listening to the tolling of bells and the somber chanting of Benedictine monks. The rain had not stopped.

She was not aware of hunger or thirst. Apart from the chanting and the rain beating on the window, she heard only one thing: *No tengas miedo,* Xochitl. Don't be afraid, Xochitl. She covered her head with the sheet and curled herself up like Athena, letting her tears and saliva soak into the futon.

She awoke to a great silence within her. When she surfaced from under the covers, she saw that her room was drenched in moonlight. The storm had passed. In the next room, her cousin was pecking at the typewriter. She got up, turned the lamp on over her bookshelf and reached for her autographed copy of *This Bridge Called My Back*, edited by two Chicana self-proclaimed dykes named Gloria Anzaldúa and Cherríe Moraga. Ivon had had the book signed by one of them when Anzaldúa visited Iowa in the Fall.

"You can't call yourself a Chicana writer if you haven't read *las maestras*," Ivon had dedicated the book.

IV.

Dear Hazel,

Today is Día de los Muertos in Mexico, an appropriate day for me to be writing this. I have been digging up Aztec history in the library, and I thought you would like to know (although, apparently, Pandora already knows) that the name Xochitl is Nahuatl for flower.

I also want to tell you that you were right. My identity does live in Mexico. I found out from nosing around in my mom's papers that we traveled from Querétaro to Ciudád Juárez in 1978. There were two train ticket stubs stuck inside an old Mexican passport that shows a picture of me and my mom, as well as a US visa with my name and age on it. Xochitl Maria Espinosa, age 10, it says. I don't know why we left and I don't remember anything about that time, except that I lived with a cousin of my mom's and a big white dog while my mom found a job in El Paso. My dad told me I got really sick after I crossed the river, a really bad fever that lasted for months and burned most of my memory away. No wonder I can't remember anything about my childhood. My dad, who is not my dad, but is the only dad I can remember, made me an American citizen when he married my mom. I was 12 and still in the fifth grade because I couldn't speak English. After I found those papers I had a dream, or maybe it was a memory disguised as a dream.

I'm in school and I can't remember the "Pledge of Allegiance," so I just move my lips and look up at the flag. But Sister Catherine—the one who changed my name to Mary—is standing behind me snapping a ruler in her hand. When the "Pledge" is finished, she tells me to take the ruler and hit myself on the mouth for lying, for pretending to know the words. I do as she tells me, and then she announces to the class that I can't say the "Pledge of Allegiance" because I'm an illegal, not a real American.

Manifest Destiny strikes again!!

One more thing. I decided to drop out of the Iowa Writer's Workshop, as it was proving to be a bad influence on my writing and moved back to El Paso to live with my dad. I'm taking a bilingual memoir class at the community college, and trying to infuse my writing with Xochitl's spirit, as you advised, which is much scarier and more painful than I could have anticipated. Sometimes, I feel as though I'm living in a twilight zone surrounded by glass piñatas.

By the way, my cousin Ricky and I are taking a train to the Copper Canyon over Spring Break. I don't have anything better to do, and it might help me improve my Spanish. It's funny, isn't it, that I used to be terrorized for not knowing English, and now I can't speak Spanish, either. I guess my spiritual guide, Gloria, would call that "pocha power."

Mil gracias for helping me break the piñata of Xochitl's identity,

Xochitl Mary Espinosa

P.S. If you don't hear from me in a year or so, please send help from the Universe.

7

"ELLA TIENE SU TONO": CONOCIMIENTO AND MESTIZA CONSCIOUSNESS IN LILIANA WILSON'S ART

"*Ella tiene su tono*: she has supernatural power from her animal soul, the *tono.*"

—Gloria Anzaldúa

Gloria Anzaldúa's auto-mytho-bio-graphical *Borderlands/La Frontera: The New Mestiza* (first published in 1987)[1] is a manual of *conocimiento*, or self-knowledge—a seven-stage process by which to awaken the mestiza inside us, whether we're male or female, queer or straight, Mexican or not. For many of my students at UCLA, Anzaldúa's concepts are too arcane and complex; for others, her writings seem simplistic, angry and condescending. The ones who "get Gloria" approach her work from an intuitive place—they are border crossers, themselves, or queers or open-hearted young people intent on learning something new rather than parroting their parents' ideologies—and they recognize in Anzaldúa's words something about themselves that they know to be true. Looking at Liliana Wilson's art gives me the same feeling as reading Anzaldúa. I become transfixed by the beauty and simplicity of the images, so immersed in her tender and tragic vision that I don't even realize something has punctured my perception, something familiar and yet alien to my awareness, as though I were looking at forgotten parts of myself. All I see are boys and girls and in-betweens occupying different terrains of grief and wonder, hope and despair, light and darkness, innocence and wisdom. I don't see the "*tono*," the animal soul that I am about to enter (Anzaldúa, 1987, 15).

Figure 4. *El día en que le hicieron pedazos la corona* by Liliana Wilson © 1991. Used by permission of the artist.

In fact, the more I study Wilson's art, the more I understand that her oeuvre is both a visual representation of the Anzaldúan program and an organic product of it. I see, in other words, the awakening of Liliana Wilson's mestiza consciousness, as described in *Borderlands/La Frontera* rendered in acrylics, colored pencils and silkscreens. I also see the artist's process of *conocimiento*, an epistemology of the self as described by Gloria Anzaldúa in some of her *Interviews*, and in her essay, "Now let us shift . . . the path of *conocimiento* . . . inner work, public acts," published in *This Bridge We Call Home* (2002). In that essay, Anzaldúa outlines the seven stages of the *conocimiento* process, which closely mirror the seven stages of mestiza consciousness I will be discussing here: Stage 1: the rupture, being shocked out of the safe zone; stage 2: Nepantla, the in-between space that is traversed when moving between states of consciousness; stage 3: the Coatlicue state, illness and plunging into "*descono-cimiento*," the falling apart stage that leads to an identity crisis, or a moment of choice; stage 4: the call to action, breaking the silence, crossing the bridge from the personal to the political; stage 5: sharing Coyolxauhqui's story, putting the pieces back together; stage 6: exploding contradictions and the uses of "love" to mitigate "the crack between worlds" (or what I call, practicing what you preach); stage 7: shifting realities and forming alliances, as in the work of spiritual activism.[2] By juxtaposing Liliana Wilson's artwork and Gloria Anzaldúa's theories on mestiza consciousness, *conocimiento*, the Shadow Beast, the Nepantla state and other border-crossing concepts, we will see how a Chilean immigrant artist and a native Chicana/*tejana* writer not only share what Adrienne Rich calls "the dream of a common language,"[3] a language rooted in sexuality, political activism, creativity and love, but also how they use this common language to guide them on their journeys toward an awakened self.

1. The Rupture, or, Locating the Border Inside Ourselves

The first stage of awakening is the sudden awareness of the border inside us, where the border is any open wound, not just the "*herida abierta* where the Third World grates against the First and bleeds" (*Borderlands* 45), but also the "*rajadura*" or crack that occurs when an outside force shatters your sense of wholeness and safety. An earthquake can cause that sudden awareness as much as a love affair or a work of art or a *coup d'état*. For Anzaldúa, it was seeing the Coyolxauhqui stone for the first time in Mexico City that showed her the different fragments of her own being, and later, the San Francisco earthquake that shattered her illusion of safety and revealed her deep-seated "fear of others breaching the walls" (Anzaldúa, "Now let us shift," 544) she had constructed around herself.

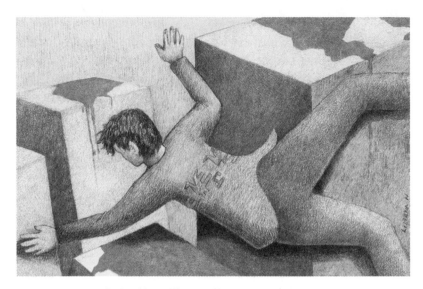

Figure 5. *City of Blood* by Liliana Wilson © 1977. Used by permission of
the artist.

For Liliana Wilson the rupture was also two-fold, as depicted
in her 1978 image *City of Blood:* first the military coup in Chile
that killed President Salvador Allende and plunged her homeland
into a war zone of torture and bloodshed, followed by her decision to immigrate to the United States and leave her family and
friends behind and become a border crosser, a citizen of Nepantla.

For those of us who were raised in *la frontera* between the
United States and Mexico, that crack, that open wound is our primary "*sitio y lengua,*" as Emma Pérez calls it, the place of origin
for our being as well as our language. That border is Nepantla[4]—
another Anzaldúan concept—the place in between two realities
that creates a third reality, a third culture or "shock culture" in-
habited by "*atrevasados*" or border crossers—"the squint-eyed,
the perverse, the queer, the troublesome, the mongrel, the mu-
latto, the half-breed, the half-dead" (*Borderlands* 25). Anybody
who is crossed in some way: racially, ethnically, linguistically,
spiritually, sexually. Anybody who contains within them the con-

tradictions of two worlds, immigrants and Chicanas/os among them, is an *"atrevasado/a."* This sudden awareness of the border inside us and the way it connects to the history of the actual geographical borderland is the first stage of consciousness. It is also an awareness of pain, since that border is "an open wound," which bleeds continually.

Figure 6. *Mujer Dividida* by Liliana Wilson © 2001. Used by permission of the artist.

In *Mujer Dividida* (2001), Liliana Wilson depicts a woman divided from herself, caught in a dark borderland of isolation with no words coming out of her mouth. "A borderland is a vague and undetermined place created by the emotional residue of an unnatural boundary" (*Borderlands* 25), says Anzaldúa. The dark background in the image signifies this "vague and undetermined place" that could represent the "unnatural boundary" between two nations, two genders, two languages or all of them at once.

For as pained as she looks, however, the woman's eyes are open, indicating that she is aware of her condition. The empty bubble in front of her face shows her that she is a non-speaking subject. She knows that she is divided, that she is wounded, but does not yet know how to speak about that pain. As Liliana Wilson says of the political conflicts in her homeland:

> Salvador Allende got elected in 1971, it was a very hopeful time for my country, but for the next three years he was attacked constantly by the military under the right wing parties, until they killed him in 1973 and took over the government. These were difficult years with all the death and torture. In 1977 I decided to leave Chile for the US. These were also difficult years because I had to leave my family and my friends, but I found myself in many other ways. For a long time I was drawing what I had seen in Chile, I was processing what had happened, while at the same time learning a new language and learning how to live here.[5]

The figures in *Memorias de Chile* (2001) and *War* (2002) do not want to face the diasporic pain of their memories, and yet the images of what they experienced and left behind continue to haunt them. They fall like dead leaves in the girl's unconscious, larger than life, or they cling like bloodstains to the boy's clothes, a skin he has shed but cannot yet release from his psyche. "I call this *desconocimiento*, being overwhelmed by reality and not wanting to confront it. *Desconocimiento* is the opposite of *conocimiento*; it's the shadow side of 'seeing,'" says Anzaldúa.[6]

2. Nepantla, or, Facing the Shadow Beast

If Nepantla is the in-between space that is traversed when moving between states of consciousness, then Nepantla is the home of the Shadow Beast. Part of the agreement that we must make as we follow Anzaldúa's snake into the dark hole of our

Figure 7. *Memorias de Chile* by Liliana Wilson © 2001. Used by permission of the artist.

unconscious is the agreement to unmask our pain, which means both to face it and to give it a face. This is the second stage of consciousness, facing the Shadow Beast that populates Nepantla and that acts as a gatekeeper to our own awareness. What is this shadowy figure that colludes with the destructive agents of self and society? Every form of internalized hatred is the Shadow Beast: racism, sexism, linguistic terrorism, homophobia. Every time we cringe when someone calls us a "*pocha*," or a "faggot," or a "dirty messcan," we take that hatred into our gut.

Tu camino de conocimiento requires that you encounter your shadow side and confront what you've programmed yourself (and have been programmed by your cultures) to avoid (*desconocer*), to confront the traits and habits distorting how you see reality and inhibiting the full use of your *facultades*. (Anzaldúa, "Now let us shift" 541)

In *Denial* (1998) the girl purposely puts her arm in front of her face to avoid looking at what is on the other side of the window at which she stands, the window itself being symbolic of a portal into another world, one that the girl is afraid to cross. "To step across the threshold is to be stripped of the illusion of safety because it moves us into unfamiliar territory and does not grant safe passage" ("Now let us shift," 3), writes Anzaldúa. The boy in *El enmasacarado* (2004) may have stepped into the dark reaches of Nepantla, but he can see only through the eyes of a false identity, the horned mask of the Shadow Beast.

Before we can enter into the Serpent and really begin this long dark journey into night, we must first face that Shadow Beast and all of the pain the Beast has caused us. We must be willing to look at the cage we have been living in, filled with false images of ourselves, like the three bird-headed figures in Wilson's ironically ti-

Figure 8. *Denial* by Liliana Wilson © 1998. Used by permission of the artist.

tled *The Meaning of Life* (1995). These false images are all reflections of the Monster we have fed too well with our secrets and fears, and the cage is our own home, our *familia*, our culture. As Anzaldúa reminds us, one way of defining homophobia is "the fear of going home" (*Borderlands* 42). Like all oppressions, homophobia begins at home. "As a person, I, as a people, we, Chicanos, blame ourselves, hate ourselves, terrorize ourselves" (*Borderlands* 67), says Anzaldúa. The fear of rejection, of denial, of ridicule, of abandonment by the mother or the family or the culture, the "agony of inadequacy"—these are only a few of the fears that hide in the cage of that Shadow Beast and that feed the Monster of internalized hatred inside every border dweller.

But that's not the only Beast that lives inside us (and this is a point too often missed by Anzaldúa scholars). There's a twin face to the Shadow Beast, not just the one who feeds off our fears and causes the pain, but the one who rebels against all that suffering, and who like the woman in *Bearing Witness* (2002), defies injustice with her third eye. This other Shadow Beast deals with

Figure 9. *El enmascarado* by Liliana Wilson © 2004. Used by permission of the artist.

Figure 10. *The Meaning of Life* by Liliana Wilson © 1995. Used by permission of the artist.

Figure 11. *Bearing Witness* by Liliana Wilson © 2002. Used by permission of the artist.

the pain by developing a seventh sense, a defiant attitude and a hard skin. Anzaldúa writes,

> There is a rebel in me—the Shadow Beast. It is a part of me that refuses to take orders from outside authorities. It refuses to take orders from my conscious will, it threatens the sovereignty of my rulership. It is that part of me that hates constraints of any kind, even those self-imposed. (*Borderlands* 38)

It is this Rebel face that goes "*soy pocha, ¿y qué?*" that doesn't allow us to shut up and stay in our place, that gets punished for being an "*hocicona*," for living out loud the contradictions that fly in the face of patriarchy and heterosexism and cultural tyranny. This face is the Hidden Other, the underfed, undernourished, but scrappy and resourceful Rebel face that strengthens rather than diminishes us. Like the girl in *La entrada al cielo* (2004), the Rebel holds the key to her own bliss. The Rebel is the opposite of the Monster, and yet it is seen as monstrous by the people who love us,

Figure 12. *La entrada al cielo* by Liliana Wilson © 2005. Used by permission of the artist.

Figure 13. *El prisionero*
by Liliana Wilson © 2004.
Used by permission of the
artist.

and whom we love despite the myriad ways in which they know-
ingly or unknowingly help us to feed the Monster of self-hate.

Like the boy in Wilson's *El prisionero* (2004), some of us
never get out of this cage, never get to see the other face of the
Shadow Beast because facing the Monster is just too painful and
we are either too afraid of the pain or too addicted to it to change
anything. As Wilson said of this image, "The cage floating over
his head is something the boy can't let go of, something keeping
him from moving forward."[7] Some of us never realize we carry
the agent of our deliverance within ourselves, and so we stay
trapped in the Monster's cage, using drugs or alcohol or sex or
any other false form of solace to help us hide from our own fear.
"Some of us take another route," says Anzaldúa. "We try to make
ourselves conscious of the Shadow Beast. . . . Yet still others of
us take it another step: we try to awaken the Shadow Beast inside
us" (*Borderlands* 42), which means listening to the voices that
have told us over and over that we are evil, unworthy and
doomed. Despite his angel wings, the boy in Wilson's *Diablitos*
(2004) is plagued by these voices, these lies about himself. He

Figure 14. *Diablitos* by
Liliana Wilson © 2005.
Used by permission of
the artist.

has not yet learned to trust that he has the power to rise above the
din, to leave the nine circles of his own inner inferno and tran-
scend his self-doubt.[8]

3. The Coatlicue State, or, Entering into the Serpent

Only when we have faced the Monster, seen through its lies,
and given a face to the Rebel can we truly say we have become
conscious of the Shadow Beast, and only then can we move on
to the third stage of consciousness and enter into the Serpent. Entering into the Serpent means surrender. It means we know the
path is covered in brambles and pitfalls, but it's the only way to
get out of our own self-manufactured traps, as the boy finds in
Organic Barbed Wire (1994). It means we trust there's a lesson
on the other side.

And we trust we have some tools that will help us brave the
hazards. One of those tools is what Anzaldúa calls "*la facultad*,"
a faculty of mind or mode of perception and survival that only

Figure 15. *Organic Barbed Wire* by Liliana Wilson © 1994. Used by permission of the artist.

those who live in the margins, those who are "other" than white, male, rich, heterosexual, Protestant, English-only US citizen norm.[9] Thus, people of color, women, the poor, queers, non-Protestants, non-English speakers and the undocumented are all margin-dwellers, and all develop *facultad*. This tool, this mode of perception, comes from deep within the arsenal of the Rebel, which is rooted in and connected to a part of the human self that for too many millennia of patriarchal dogma[10] has been trod underfoot, like the snake: the feminine principle. *La facultad*, in other words, is one of the ways of knowing attributed to women and ridiculed by men. Connected to the esoteric knowledge represented by the night and the moon, *la facultad* is akin to intuition, instinct and the natural world. It is an irrational form of knowing, what Anzaldúa calls a "subversive knowledge" ("Now let us shift," 542) existing outside of the linear dimension known as logic, and for that reason useless to a mind socially constructed to devalue women, nature and the body. To resist *la facultad*,

Figure 16. *El ridículo* by
Liliana Wilson © 2005.
Used by permission of
the artist.

however, is to be tied up under a dunce cap, as in Liliana Wilson's
El ridículo (2005). How often do we regret not heeding our intuition and finding ourselves caught up in a dangerous or ridicu-
lous situation that we could have avoided had we "listened to our
gut," that is, paid attention to our *facultad*?

> Whatever it was that was the wrong thing to do—an
> obsession of some kind, probably—the boy trapped him-
> self. The answer was in the universe but he couldn't see
> it. He made a fool of himself. He's still not looking at it,
> he's crying but his eyes are downcast.[11]

Surrendering to the serpent means letting ourselves go fully
into Nepantla, "the point of contact where the 'mundane' and the
'numinous' converge, where you're in full awareness of the present moment" (Anzaldúa, "Now let us shift," 549). From this in-
between place, it is possible to see all of the contradictions that

have been raging inside us, threatening to burn down the false structure in which we have housed our identity, as we see happening to Wilson's *Mujer desesperada* (2000).

"We can't continue to believe the mental constructions that male society has built for women," says Wilson (telephone interview, 29 September 2008). Anzaldúa argues that part of the process of *conocimiento* is learning to distinguish between "*lo impuesto, lo adquirido*, and *lo heredado*" (*Borderlands* 104)— or rather, learning to see through the social constructions we have inherited, acquired or had imposed on us by our culture. It's like looking in a mirror and seeing three reflections of the self: the self you think you have to be, the self that others construct and the self that reflects your own fears and desires. A woman's place is in the home, stand by your man, be a good mother—these men-

Figure 17. *Mujer desesperada* by Liliana Wilson © 1999. Used by permission of the artist.

Figure 18. *Muerte en la frontera* by Liliana Wilson © 2007. Used by permission of the artist.

tal constructions are images we have inherited from our culture, from generations of oppressed and repressed women before us, who were socialized to believe they had no agency but to serve patriarchal needs and interests. Wetback, welfare mom, cleaning lady, bad girl, whore—these are reflections imposed on women of color from the outside and duplicated in popular culture as we see in *Muerte en la frontera* (2007) where the young victims of vicious femicides are held responsible for their own deaths. As these imposed and inherited ideologies go up in smoke for *Mujer desesperada*, she sees yet another reflection, the one that shows her how terrified she really is of being alone, like the woman in *The Wedding* (1996). In this reflection she sees how she has contributed to her own desperation and sense of failure by acquiring habits and addictions that do nothing more than enable the possessive fantasies of patriarchy and capitalism.

Figure 19. *The Wedding* by Liliana Wilson © 1995. Used by permission of the artist.

This, in turn, Anzaldúa explains, only blocks the natural process of molting.

> Held in thrall by one's obsession, by the god or goddess symbolizing that addiction, one is not empty enough to become possessed by anything else. One's attention cannot be captured by something else, one does not "see" and awareness does not happen. One remains ignorant of the fact that one is afraid, and that it is fear that holds one petrified, frozen in stone. If we can't see the face of fear in the mirror, then fear must not be there. (*Borderlands* 67)

Here Anzaldúa shows us the problem as well as the solution: to divest ourselves of the distractions we've been using to cope with or hide from our reality, and to allow ourselves to become possessed by our fears and contradictions. To fully face the mirror and see that: I am a woman in a patriarchal, misogynistic society, a lesbian in a heterosexist culture, a Mexican in a country that despises Mexicans. I speak Spanish forked by the tongue of my Anglo colonizer. I want to liberate my Raza and my body, which my own people seek to imprison and control. Like Alice stepping through the looking glass into a world of double consciousness where objects and animals can speak and where her own politics of location are tested, we must step through the "*rajadura*" in the mirror to reach the other side of Nepantla, the place of transformation that we see depicted in *La Llegada* (1997).

To empty ourselves of our negative behaviors and distractions is to surrender to that voice that speaks to us from the darkness, a voice that leads us to the dangerous precipice of *conocimiento*. In the eternal now that is Nepantla, where the ma-

Figure 20. *La llegada* by Liliana Wilson © 1997. Used by permission of the artist.

terial world and the spirit world converge, it is possible to commune with ghosts and serpents, and it is also possible to meet the internal destructive and creative energy that is represented by Coatlicue, the mother of the Aztec gods, goddess of creation and death. It will be Coatlicue that pushes us to betray our deepest secret. Anzaldúa writes in *Borderlands* "The secret I tried to conceal was that I was not normal, that I was not like the others. I felt alien. I knew I was alien. I was the mutant stoned out of the herd" (*Borderlands* 65). In *La caída del ángel* (2005), Liliana Wilson shows a fallen angel covering his face in shame or sorrow. Whether he is cast out from his community in the heavens and doomed to a solitary existence for all time, or whether he is burdened by loss, his heavy wings keep him immobilized. At this point, the crisis begins, the catatonic period of *"desconocimiento"* that is an essential, albeit terrifying and agonizing, aspect of the Coatlicue state. For some of us, this is the longest and most difficult stage in the process of awakening.

> Cast adrift from all that's familiar, you huddle deep in the womb cave, a stone repelling light. In the void of your own nothingness, you lie in a fetal curl clutching the fragmented pieces and bits of yourself you've disowned. (Anzaldúa, "Now let us shift" 551)

What characterizes this phase of the Coatlicue state is immobility, brought on by physical or psychic illness that catalyzes those fears and contradictions into a crisis of identity. The Coatlicue state is a necessary moment in our process of "making soul," a time of stasis and reflection in which we see both the horror and the beauty of our Nepantla existence. This clear seeing from what Anzaldúa calls the "reptilian eye" in the middle of the forehead, also shows us that we have a choice, for indeed, choice, or rather the ability to decide, is the etymological root of the word "crisis."[12] By focusing on the destructive aspects of a

Figure 21. *La caída del ángel* by Liliana Wilson © 2004. Used by permission of the artist.

crisis, the falling apart stage, we overlook the fact that a crisis is actually a moment of choice, when all of our options—the disowned pieces of the self—overwhelm us at once and we must exercise our power to choose what to do to bring the self back together, or to restructure the self. Wikipedia defines crisis as "a traumatic or stressful change in a person's life, or an unstable and dangerous social situation, in political, social, economic, military affairs, or a large-scale environmental event, especially one involving an impending abrupt change."[13] Certainly, leaving one's homeland produces a traumatic and stressful change in an immigrant's life, even more a political overthrow.

Talking about *La caída del ángel,* Liliana Wilson explains that the fallen angel has "come through something really horrible and doesn't realize he's survived; he thinks he's still in that other place," and connects it to her own Coatlicue state while still in Chile, when the military took over. "They wiped out the old

Chile, they were demons, I was living in Hell. Our own Chilean people were doing that to us." Not only did she *desconocer*, or fail to recognize, her homeland, but also she lost touch with her sense of herself as a Chilean. Another Coatlicue state happened when she first arrived in the United States: "I left everything and I just jumped into another world completely. It was pretty *despedazante*. It tore me up. All the pieces of me were left behind. I had to rebuild myself completely, like I was born again" (telephone interview, 29 September 2008).

4. Breaking the Silence/Call to Action

Overcoming silence is the fourth stage of *conocimiento*, whether the silence is the result of military repression, domestic abuse, homophobia or what Anzaldúa calls "linguistic terrorism," that despotic nationalism in both the United States and Mexico that insists you must speak only English or only Spanish, and that punishes and ridicules you for speaking both languages at once. Chicanas and Chicanos who are embarrassed that they don't "speak Spanish correctly," or that they speak Spanglish rather than English-only, who flinch at being called "*pochos*" and "*pochas*,"[14] are suffering the effects of this linguistic terror campaign that is enforced by Mexican nationals on both sides of the border. Similarly, children who are punished at school for speaking Spanish, or who are tracked into "special education" classes or vocational classes because they don't speak English or speak it with a heavy accent are also suffering from cultural and linguistic violence. Enforced at home and at school, this violence becomes internalized, and is another way of feeding the monstrous side of the Shadow Beast. A popular slogan in the gay community is "silence=death," because to be silent is to collude with our oppressors, is to patently accept their violations as part of the status quo, and therefore, to condone them. "It's dangerous," says Liliana Wilson. "The war is happening, and it has not stopped happening. So I talk about it without talking about it. That's how

I paint" (telephone interview, 29 September 2008). Art is Liliana Wilson's tool for breaking the silence, for navigating the identity crises of her Coatlicue state, and for creating bridges between her past and her present, her politics and her spirituality.

In the Fall of 1995, Liliana Wilson and Gloria Anzaldúa came together for "El Taller Nepantla," (Nepantla Workshop), a 5-week residency that brought five Latina artists, writers and painters from both sides of the border, to the Saratoga Hills near San Jose, California to explore Anzaldúa's concept of Nepantla— "the idea of entering a place between the extremes of their cultures"[15] —in their work. In Mexico, it was a time of civil unrest as the Zapatista Liberation Army was simultaneously protesting the neocolonial invasion of the North American Free Trade Agreement, demanding their rights as autonomous Mexican citizens while being massacred by their own government.[16] In California, once the panacea of liberal thinkers and civil rights activists, voters had just passed Proposition 187 the year before, which denied such basic human rights as health care and education to the undocumented, the first of a trifecta of civil rights backlashes in the state that would ban Affirmative Action in 1996 (Proposition 209) and Bilingual Education in 1998 (Proposition 227).

"We're here to make order out of this chaos, we're here to make meaning," Anzaldúa said in an interview. "This act of making meaning I call Nepantla" (Reynolds 1995). It was here that Liliana Wilson crossed one of her own internal borders and added a new subject to her paintings.

> We [were] walking in the woods every day and talking about our ideas. I'[d] been painting a lot of images of men up until [then], I think because I [could] be kind of distant from them. But [since then], I've started painting girls. (quoted in Reynolds 1995)

Part of what motivated her to avoid portraying women and girls in her work, Liliana Wilson told me, is that she didn't want

Figure 22. *Girl and Red Fish*
by Liliana Wilson © 1994.
Used by permission of the
artist.

to "victimize" them, but she also wanted to show male figures as "more vulnerable, to represent my own pain" (personal interview, 22 March 2008). Rendering her pain onto male figures was a way of detaching herself from the memory of those feelings.

For Anzaldúa, it was storytelling that gave her the power to "battle the silence and the red. Daily I take my throat in my hands and squeeze until the cries pour out, my larynx and soul sore from the constant struggle" (*Borderlands* 93-94). For in telling the story of "the red," which signifies her pain, Anzaldúa both re-lives and releases the illness caused by the pain. Writing, then, simultaneously immerses her in the Coatlicue state, gives meaning to her experience and restores her to health.

When I write it feels like I am carving bone. It feels like I'm creating my own face, my own heart—a Nahuatl concept. My soul makes itself through the creative act. It is constantly remaking and giving birth to itself through my body. It is this learning to live with la Coatlicue that transforms living in the Borderlands from a nightmare to a numinous experience. It is always a path/state to something else. (*Borderlands* 95)[17]

That "something else" is the epistemology of the self that Anzaldúa calls *conocimiento*, and once tapped, the healing of the severed parts can begin.

5. Putting the Pieces Together, or, Making Coyolxauhqui Whole Again

Coyolxauhqui is your symbol for both the process of emotional and psychic dismemberment, splitting body/ mind/spirit/ soul, and the creative work of putting all the pieces together in a new form, a partially unconscious work done in the night by the light of the moon, a labor of re-visioning and re-membering. (Anzaldúa, "Now let us shift" 546)

For Liliana Wilson, it was art-making that allowed her to put the pieces back together. Art was her calling as well as her way of healing the psychic splits and open wounds that were the consequence of her exile. Making art allowed her to "revision and remember": to expose the rapacious agendas and rabid dangers of living in a military dictatorship, as we see in *La junta de gobierno* (1995).
To reflect on what it felt like growing up in a family made dysfunctional by alcoholism and machismo, as we see in the ironic portrayal of *Successful Family* (1999).
To show the helplessness of an immigrant coming to a country that despises immigrants, as we see in *Proposition 187* (1998).

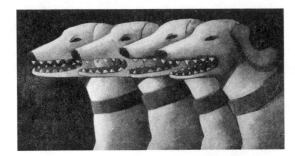

Figure 23. *La junta de gobierno* by Liliana Wilson © 1995. Used by permission of the artist.

Figure 24. *The Successful Family* by Liliana Wilson © 1999. Used by permission of the artist.

Figure 25. *Proposition 187* by Liliana Wilson © 1998. Used by permission of the artist. In the collection of Alicia Gaspar de Alba.

And to depict the despair caused by a culture based on corporate
greed and violence, particularly against women and children, as
we see in *Greed* (2003).

Figure 26. *Greed* by Liliana Wilson © 2003. Used by permission of the
artist.

As the artist, Wilson sees through the experience, and this seeing
"enrages" her, and fuels her desire for change, but her images are
rarely brutal or political. "I transform rage into a real deep sorrow,"
she says. "The military in Chile was so horrendous, that I got the
point that rage or protest gets you nowhere, we can't tell the truth
because we'll pay for it, we have to be smart enough to say the
truth without being obvious and calling the attention of those who
would hurt us" (telephone interview, 29 September 2008).

Although painful and isolating, loss and the subsequent crisis that loss produces, is a necessary part of *conocimiento*—in
Liliana's case, loss of language, family, country, identity—for
this is what Anzaldúa means by the process of molting, of shed-
ding skins, which implies growth and transformation. Out of *desconocimiento*, comes consciousness, Anzaldúa reminds us. Out of
the shattered self comes the whole. In *Sábila Sagrada* (2008) the
girl sits serenely in a garden holding a potted aloe vera plant that

Figure 27. *Sábila sagrada* by Liliana Wilson © 2008. Used by permission of the artist.

signifies a healed self, centered in a life of beauty and connection to the natural world.

6. The Methodology of Love

It is through her painting that Liliana Wilson gives voice to the Rebel inside her who is not afraid to depict the horrors, the hypocrisies and the sorrows of a political refugee's life. And yet, despite the painful situations that she paints, her human figures are always innocent and fragile. Even amidst the despair, there is some form of beauty, in the wise and gentle eyes of her androgynous boys and girls, in the lush plants and flowers of her landscapes, in the moonlit and starlit skies of her universes. The naked woman in *La bella durmiente* (2004), whose title evokes the fairy tale of "Sleeping Beauty," sleeps safely under an open window, unafraid of the night. Like Anzaldúa for whom darkness and the night represent "the mystery of the Origin" (*Borderlands* 71), Lil-

Figure 28. *La bella durmiente* by Liliana Wilson © 2004. Used by permission of the artist.

iana Wilson exercises her own subversive knowledge of this mystery by finding the nugget of gold in every painful experience.

"If I were to just depict the pain and not the beauty, nobody would want to look at my work, nobody would want to have it. What I want to give is love, only with love can we begin to heal" (telephone interview, 29 September 2008), says Wilson.

Chicana theorist Chela Sandoval calls love part of the "methodology of the oppressed," both the means by which to change the world and the change itself. It is a revolutionary not a romantic love meant to instigate social change, an "oppositional social act." "It is love that can access and guide our theoretical and political '*movidas*'" writes Sandoval, "—revolutionary maneuvers toward decolonized being."[18] Sandoval believes that Third World revolutionaries such as Anzaldúa, Emma Pérez, Cherríe Moraga and Che Guevara all "understand love as a 'breaking' through whatever controls us in order to find 'understanding and community': it is described as 'hope' and 'faith' in the potential goodness of some promised land" (Sandoval 140).

Although the young immigrant in *El color de la esperanza* (1987) has survived countless travails to reach the border of the so-called promised land, where they will be poached on by "*coyotes*" and hunted down by the Border Patrol, they trust that their faith will protect them and their dreams of a better life fill them with love and hope.

Figure 29. *El color de la esperanza* by Liliana Wilson © 1987. Used by permission of the artist.

Twenty years later, Wilson continues to depict understanding and community in the hope of immigrant survival. She describes *La espera* (2007) as the story of a mother waiting for a son who will never come back. "Who knows where he's gone, maybe the war, maybe the United States, but he's not coming back to her"

Figure 30. *La espera* by
Liliana Wilson © 2007.
Used by permission of the
artist.

(telephone interview, 29 September 2008), says Wilson. Nothing
can shake the woman's conviction that she will see her son again,
and like so many mothers of immigrants and soldiers, she waits
for him to make his presence felt, undefeated by despair, her hope
flowering abundantly all around her. Perhaps she feels him in the
fluttering wings of the hummingbird, or "in a slither of serpents"
(*Borderlands* 73) whispering his name. Although she is resigned
to the loss, she will never stop waiting for him.

7. Mestiza Consciousness/Spiritual Activism

For Anzaldúa and Wilson, love as a methodology by which to
explode contradictions and mitigate "the crack between worlds"
gives them the ability, the *poder* or power, to "shift realities and

form alliances," which leads to the seventh and final stage in the process of *conocimiento*, "mestiza consciousness."

Although related to José Vasconcelos' ideology of a fifth race forged by the biological blending of the four major races of humanity—Caucasian, Indian, African and Asian—to form a "bronze" hybrid that the Mexican secretary of education termed "*raza cósmica*,"[19] Anzaldúa's "mestiza" is more than a biological hybrid, more than a bridge between races whose purpose was to "redeem the dark races" (Vasconcelos 20). Anzaldúa gives us a "new mestiza," an "alien consciousness . . . a consciousness of the Borderlands . . . una *conciencia de mujer*" (*Borderlands* 99). Anzaldúa argues that a new consciousness can be created the way a new race is created, by joining opposites, by mixing the male with the female, the black with the white, the English with the Spanish, the Anglo with the Mexican, the body with the spirit, the subject with the object. In this way does the New Mestiza "sustain contradictions" and create "a tolerance for ambiguity" that never has to choose between two opposing sides, but rather stands "on both shores at once and, at once, see[s] through serpent and eagle eyes" (*Borderlands* 101-100). Unlike Vasconcelos whose eugenic dream was to create a cosmic melting pot for the melding of One exclusive universal race, the New Mestiza is a consciousness of inclusivity in which "nothing is thrust out, the good, the bad, and the ugly, nothing rejected, nothing abandoned" (*Borderlands* 101).

Like Liliana Wilson's *El dividido* (2004), the New Mestiza is aware that she bridges opposites and contradictions. Wilson described this piece as the "universe being outside and within the boy, everything that is contained in the universe has always existed" (telephone interview, 29 September 2008). The blue and red, as opposite qualities in the color spectrum—cold and hot, tranquility and passion—represent two separate worlds, or two shores, and the boy stands between both of them, not split and isolated, but cleaved to his own duality, standing on both shores at once, all of his contradictions contained. In Nepantla nothing

Figure 31. *El dividido*
by Liliana Wilson ©
2004. Used by permis-
sion of the artist.

is certain, but the boy's peaceful expression shows that he has learned "tolerance for ambiguity." Indeed, the boy appears to be drifting in this ambiguous universe, what Chela Sandoval would call the "no-place of the abyss," that utopian state of being in which "subjectivity can become freed from ideology as it binds and ties reality; here is where political weapons of consciousness are available in a constant tumult of possibility" (Sandoval 142).

Like *Los ilusionistas* (2007), the New Mestiza "learns to juggle cultures," as Anzaldúa tells us in *Borderlands*, and this juggling is a constant shifting of locations and languages, or "*sitios y lenguas*," a "continual creative motion that keeps breaking down the unitary aspect of each new paradigm" (*Borderlands* 102). The figures here could be boys, could be girls, could be hermaphrodites or spirits. What they are doing is impossible in the world of gravity, but that is not their world. Theirs is a universe of possi-

Figure 32. *Los ilusionistas* by Liliana Wilson © 2005. Used by permission of the artist

bility and playfulness, where nothing is impractical or unattainable, worthless or useless. It is here in the delicate balance of left brain and right brain, root chakra and crown chakra, positive and negative, day and night, yin and yang, male and female, straight and queer, here in this place of constantly shifting locations and languages that the New Mestiza finds the bridge she calls home.

The New Mestiza is both *Leonardo* (2007)—beloved of the wild creatures who radiates light from his left hand, a boy "so pure he floats on water," as Wilson describes him, and the girl in *Transformación* (2004), whose rebirth happens in the liminal space between sea and sky where her fragmented selves blossom into a third element.

Figure 33. *Leonardo* by Liliana Wilson © 2009. Used by permission of the artist.

"In attempting to work out a synthesis," Anzaldúa writes, "the self has added a third element which is greater than the sum of its severed parts. That third element is a new consciousness—a *mestiza* consciousness" (*Borderlands* 102). The stargazer lily represents the element of earth, and signifies both the feminine principle that gives birth to her artistic creations and the spiritual power that connects us to the natural world, but it is also symbolic of the artist's own name, Liliana, gazing at stars, growing stars. *Ella tiene su tono.*

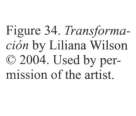

Figure 34. *Transformación* by Liliana Wilson © 2004. Used by permission of the artist.

8
BAD GIRLS RISE AGAIN:
THE *SINFUL SAINTS* & *SAINTLY SINNERS* AT
THE *MARGINS OF THE AMERICAS* EXHIBITION

Figure 35. *Our Lady* by
Alma Lopez © 1999.
Digital print on canvas.
Used by permission of
the artist.

Bikini Virgins of Guadalupe are no strangers to Santa Fe,
New Mexico, despite the holy hoopla that the city's devout
Catholic community stirs up over these representations. In the
Santa Fe Reporter's online "Summer Guide 2013," for example,
the cover was a bikini-clad, margarita-sipping Virgen de

Guadalupe in sunglasses flanked by tourists, cowboys and eternal children. Of course, many of us remember the first representation of the Virgen de Guadalupe to cause such a stir in the City of Holy Faith in 2001, Alma Lopez's digital collage, *Our Lady*, called "Our Lady of All This Fuss" and "Our Lady of Controversy" in the popular media. What outraged the fundamentalist Catholics who protested the image was the photograph of a very self-assured Latina woman standing barefoot in contrapposto, in a two-piece composed of roses. It wasn't just her muscular abs and quads or her confrontational attitude that scandalized all those good Catholics who wanted to censor the work from the exhibition in which it was being featured and crucify the artist for good measure, but also that Our Lady was held aloft by a bare-breasted female angel with the wings of a Viceroy butterfly. This combination of a defiant rather than a submissive Virgin, an angel with exposed breasts and a pierced nipple, and a human rather than abstract or caricature representation of the Virgen launched a controversy that stretched from Santa Fe to Philadelphia and traveled even more broadly on the worldwide web.

The uproar lasted for nine months and reverberated on the Internet for ten years, culminating in a book, which I co-edited with Alma, titled *Our Lady of Controversy: Alma López's "Irreverent Apparition."* The book's publication and the exhibition of *Our Lady* on the walls of the Oakland Museum of California and at University College Cork, Ireland (all of which took place in 2011), reignited the flames of outrage that had been lit to immolate the artist ten years earlier sparked by the right-wing reactionary group from Pennsylvania, America Needs Fatima (ANF), and adroitly fanned by the Catholic Church.

Although the ANF never poked its nose into the ferment surrounding the "bikini Virgin" of 2013, protestors once again stirred the fundamentalist coals over which Alma Lopez was raked back in 2001. Enrique Limón makes this patently clear in his interview with Alma published in the *Santa Fe Reporter*, "Shame As It Ever

Was: Twelve Years after 'Our Lady' Controversy, Artist Alma López Looks Back."[1] Whether she intended her artwork to provoke or not, it is undeniable that Lopez's *Our Lady* has been woven into the popular culture of Santa Fe. If there's anything the *Santa Fe Reporter's* article proves, it is to what degree this "bad girl," and the artist who conceptualized her, continue to cast a huge shadow over New Mexico.

Because of her controversial reputation, Alma Lopez was invited to participate in the 2013 *Sinful Saints & Saintly Sinners at the Margins of the Americas* exhibition at the Fowler Cultural History Museum in Los Angeles. The curator, Patrick Polk, was especially interested in including her print of another controversial cultural figure, Juan Soldado—the secular patron saint of border crossers. Unlike the legendary Virgen de Guadalupe, Soldado was a real person as well as a cultural icon with a contentious history. To the immigrants who visit his shrine in Tijuana and lay candles and other offerings at his feet (and even at his paraffin representation at the Tijuana Wax Museum), he is the miraculous soldier-saint who will get them safely across the border. To his critics, he is a child molester, rapist and murderer. Lopez, however, playing off the popular devotion of her own immigrant nation, has repackaged Soldado as a modern-day manifestation of Coyolxauhqui, the Aztec warrior goddess, who is said to have been dismembered and beheaded by her brother, Huitzilopochtli, the god of war. By placing an image of the goddess behind that of Juan Soldado, Lopez assigns him a similar status as a protective warrior. She also calls attention to a further parallel between the Aztec deity and the soldier. Just as Coyolxauhqui may not have sought so much to murder her mother and betray her brother as to defend her people against the warfare and bloodshed that would ensue under Huitzilopochtli's rule as the God of War, Juan Soldado also may have been misrepresented, framed for a crime that many still do not think him capable of committing. But the dismembered sister at his back may, at the same time, signify the victims of physical

violence, the forgotten remains of raped and murdered sisters that
are never pieced together and that Lopez memorializes each time
she infuses Coyolxauhqui into one of her works.

Why and how Juan Soldado became the secular patron saint
of border crossers remains top-secret;[2] even more mysterious is
how Lopez's rendition of Juan Soldado has become integrated
into the votive iconography of the saint, alongside more traditional representations of the uniformed soldier and other popular
religious icons and prayer cards sold outside of Tijuana's Pan-
teón #1, where the Juan Soldado shrine is located.

Indeed, Lopez's representation has been made into other religious paraphernalia, including an ex-voto tile, cemented into

Figure 36. *Juan Soldado* by Alma Lopez © 1997. Digital print on vinyl.
Used by permission of the artist.

the brick wall of the shrine by a believer from Guadalajara in gratitude for a granted favor. "I think it's pretty cool that it's my rendition of Juan Soldado that people are praying to these days," Lopez remarked in a personal conversation with me. "It really shows how it's the people who create their own saints, because they need them, they need to reconcile dichotomies in their lives, and they create saints to help them do that" (personal communication, 2013). The Los Angeles skyline that looms behind Lopez's representation of Juan Soldado points to the huge number of Mexican immigrants who populate the city's landscape. "They are all in need of a mediator who can help them navigate the complex issues of migration, residency, and citizenship," the artist adds. She clarifies that her Juan Soldado holds the green card of her younger brother, the only one of her siblings who is still not a citizen. "I feel Juan Soldado has intervened on my brother's behalf because he's almost been deported several times."

Juan Soldado forms part of Lopez's series *1848: Chicanos/Latinos in the U.S. Landscape after the Signing of the Treaty of Guadalupe-Hidalgo*, which consists of five digital prints on paper and on canvas created between 1997 and 1999. These prints interrogate the anti-immigrant policies and immigrant-bashing propaganda of former California governor Pete Wilson. During Wilson's tenure, the following were passed: Proposition 187, which denied access to public education, health care and other social services for undocumented immigrants; Proposition 209, which completely undermined affirmative action legislation; and Proposition 227, which ended bilingual education in public schools. Each piece in the *1848* series,[3] features a background depicting the Los Angeles skyline, a historical map of the Mexican north at the time of the signing of the Treaty of Guadalupe Hidalgo in 1848,[4] the present-day Tijuana-San Diego border fence, and a tagged mural of the Virgen de Guadalupe at the lower right corner. Layered over this border history, *Juan Soldado* and the other pieces in the series counter stereotypes of the "illegal" Mexican in the United States and the idea that Mexican immigrants are invading and living like leeches off the resources of others. Perhaps like Juan Soldado, himself, Mexican (and other Latinx) immigrants, already labeled "wetbacks and "illegals," have always been synonymous with "criminals."

Three paintings from Lopez's 2010 *Queer Santas* series— *Santa Lucia, Santa Liberata* and *Saint Wilgefortis*—represent what I term "framed bodies," that is, bodies of women accused of crimes they did not commit and blamed for their own horrible deaths. Adapting the form of the circus banner for these works, the artist underscores the perceived "freakish" nature of young women who refuse heterosexual marriage in patriarchy. Lopez rewrites the "martyr" narrative of each Catholic saint that is used to explain or justify the deadly violence perpetrated on each young female body for rejecting the biological imperative of her sex, and in essence asks, "What kind of woman would rather be tortured to death than have to marry a man?" The queer answer, of course, is "a lesbian." Thus, Lopez reveals the queer nature of these so-called Catholic martyrs, who supposedly sacrificed themselves to consecrate their virginity to Jesus Christ.

Santa Lucia, an Italian saint of the late third and early fourth century, was a noblewoman punished for refusing to marry a pagan during the period when Emperor Diocletian was persecuting the early Christians. She was thrown into a brothel, tortured and had her eyes gouged out. Representations of Saint Lucía usually depict her holding a plate with her eyeballs on it, and she is now regarded as the patron saint of the blind. Alma Lopez's *Santa Lucía* holds her eyeballs in her palms like stigmata. She also wears a *bandolero* of roses that signify the traditional *soldadera*, or soldier woman, of the Mexican Revolution. *Santa Lucía* is thus imbued with a warrior nature and a history of resistance against colonialism and mysogyny. The roses, however, also refer to and connect Santa Lucía with another framed body in Alma Lopez's

Figure 37. *Santa Lucía* by Alma Lopez © 2011. Acrylic on canvas. (Special thanks to Cristina Serna). Used by permission of the artist.

oeuvre: *Our Lady*. Rather than the narrative of violence represented by the bullets worn by *soldaderas*, the roses demonstrate the narrative of love that underscores Lopez's transformation of the Virgin of Guadalupe and these martyred female saints.

Santa Liberata, the Italian name for Saint Wilgefortis, is a second-century martyr who shared a similar fate as a persecuted Christian. According to the legend, Wilgefortis/Liberata was the daughter of the king of Portugal, who wanted to marry her off to a pagan king. Unbeknownst to her father, Wilgefortis/Liberata was a secret Christian, and she prayed that Jesus Christ would liberate her from this marriage by making her ugly. In answer to her prayers, the legend goes, a full beard sprouted on the young girl's face. The marriage was called off, and the enraged king had his defiant daughter crucified. Thus, Liberata/Wilgefortis is represented as a bearded female saint hanging on a cross (although some believe the image is that of the Volto Santo, or crucified Christ figure wearing a gown rather than a loincloth). Liberata/ Wilgefortis became a cult figure in the fourteenth century, the patron saint of unwanted or abusive marriages, and her cult extended from Germany, Portugal and Spain to Brazil and other parts of the colonial Americas. In 1969, Vatican II suppressed her cult and removed her feast day from the calendar of saints' days, thereby erasing her from the Catholic family.

Lopez enlisted Chicana lesbian feminists, Emma Pérez and yours truly, who identify as "butch" women, to serve as models for her Liberata and Wilgefortis interpretations, respectively. Lopez underscores the queer nature of this saint, her transnational and transhistorical rebelliousness. This is echoed in the appearance of the artist's print *Our Lady de Coyolxauqhi*[5] on Liberata's tank top and the shield bearing the crown, sword and fleur-de-lis reminiscent of Joan of Arc, on the shirt of Wilgefortis. In the background of the latter painting is a screen print taken from a stained-glass window of the bearded saint herself, palms nailed to a cross, waist and legs bound by rope, standing atop a pile of wood like a witch about to be burnt at the stake.

Like the thirteenth-century Aztec warrior goddess Coyolxauhqui, Joan of Arc was also a warrior woman. A peasant girl who heard the voices of angels instructing her to protect the kingdom of France, she led the French army in bloody battles against the English invaders in the fifteenth century during the Hundred Years' War. By connecting Coyolxauhqui and Joan of Arc historically to the second century Wilgefortis/Liberata, Lopez establishes a genealogy of rebel women, sinful women in the eyes of their communities, who dared to defy the patriarchal gender codes that would have limited them to roles as wives, mothers or courtesans. Each is a "framed body," blamed for bringing about her own demise. Coyolxauhqui is blamed for daring to raise a hand to her mother, Coatlicue, the great goddess of life and death.

Figure 38. *Santa Liberata* by Alma Lopez © 2011. Acrylic on canvas. (Special thanks to Emma Pérez). Used by permission of the artist.

Figure 39. *St. Wilgefortis* by Alma Lopez © 2011. Acrylic on canvas. (Special thanks to Alicia Gaspar de Alba). Used by permission of the artist.

Figure 40. *Our Lady Coyolx-auhqui* by Alma Lopez ©
2011. Silkscreen. Used by
permission of the artist.

Joan of Arc was put on trial and found guilty of witchcraft for
heeding the voices of angels and wearing male clothes. Wilge-
fortis/Liberata prayed to be made ugly and sprouted a beard.
Lucia defied the Roman emperor with her Christian faith and was
blinded. Playing with the notion of saints as circus freaks—the
bearded lady, the eyeless woman, the dismembered sister and the
butch lesbian—Lopez uses her *Queer Santas* series to invert the
traditional narrative of the Christian conversion story. Rather than
consecrating their virginity to Jesus Christ, Alma Lopez's *santas*
protect their virginity as a sign of their queer identity.

　　Gloria Anzaldúa's book *Borderlands/La Frontera* was a primary influence for the *1848* series; Lopez explains that what most
resonated for her was the author's notion of *"atravesados"* (*Borderlands* 3), that is, those who dwell in between two nations, gen-

ders, languages and sexualities. Indeed, Lopez transformed a quotation from Anzaldúa, "this is her home/this thin edge of/barbwire" (*Borderlands*, 13) into another piece in the *1848* series, *La Línea*, which depicts a young girl jumping playfully along the border fence, balancing on the razor-thin line that separates the United States and Mexico, which is a vast historical and cultural expanse. For the bilingual, bicultural queers who tread that thin line, one strategy of survival, as Lopez sees it, is to invent their own saints and intermediaries. *Santa Niña de Mochis* is for the orphans and Dreamers north of the border, and *Our Lady* for the politicized, educated, self-aware Chicana feminists often ostracized by their own families and community.

Another artist whose work resonates with Gloria Anzaldúa's border theories is the Chilean Liliana Wilson. In another essay in this volume, *"Ella Tiene Su Tono: Conocimiento* and Mestiza Consciousness in Liliana Wilson's Art," I compare Wilson's oeuvre to Gloria Anzaldúa's template for achieving a borderlands consciousness by engaging in a tumultuous process of self-knowledge to show how the politics of place represented by a military coup in the artist's homeland is presented as a series of crossings that encompass geographical, political, spiritual and sexual borders. I connect Wilson's imagery to the border-crossing experience of *pochos*,[6] halfbreeds, *atravesados* and queers that Anzaldúa folds into the frame of *"la nueva mestiza,"* or rather, mestiza consciousness, the consciousness that integrates opposites, tolerates ambiguities and embodies contradictions, rather than choosing a binary existence.

Anzaldúa's predominant metaphor for this new consciousness is the serpent: the earthbound reptile that molts out of its skin and grows a new one each year; the metaphoric snake that, like our *conocimiento*, or inner knowledge, spirals in and out of different stages of awareness; and the spiritual snake that connects her to the transformative power of the Aztec fertility goddesses Cihuacoatl and Coatlicue. "The snake is a symbol of awakening consciousness . . . [t]he potential of knowing within, an awareness and intelligence not grasped by logical thought" (Anzaldúa, 2002, 540). That awakening, that intelligence, comes through the body, through the sexuality of the body. For Anzaldúa, the serpent is a feminine energy: "she, the symbol of the dark sexual drive, the chthonic (underworld), the feminine, the serpentine movement of sexuality, of creativity, the basis of all energy and life" (*Borderlands* 57). Although Anzaldúa suffered a near-fatal snakebite as a young girl, and saw visions of serpents throughout her life, it took her years of consciousness work to connect with her animal soul. "Forty years it's taken me to enter into the Serpent, to acknowledge that I have a body, that I am a body, and to assimilate the animal body, the animal soul" (*Borderlands* 48).

In *Eva* (2005) Liliana Wilson shows us a different version of the Biblical story of Eve, the original "bad girl" of the Bible. Rather than depicting the serpent as a symbol of evil, and Eve as a humiliated woman who is cast out of Eden not only for disobeying God's orders not to eat of the sacred tree of knowledge but also for tempting Adam to partake in the same sin, Wilson's *Eva* is a woman at ease in her naked female body, a body that

Figure 41. *Eva* by Liliana Wilson © 2005. Used by permission of the artist.

rather than demonizing the serpent, has assimilated the animal body of the serpent, and thus the inner knowing of her creative root, her sexual desire that comes from the animal soul. There is no shame or penitence in *Eva*. Wearing the seashell that connects her to the mysteries of the ocean and standing under the full moon that guides her into the mysteries of the night, this "bad girl" holds the snake of her own *conocimiento* in her hands. As Anzaldúa would have described it, she "takes dominion over serpents—over [her] own body, [her] sexual activity, [her] soul, [her] mind, [her] weaknesses and strengths" (*Borderlands* 73). Liliana Wilson's *Eva* is a *nueva mestiza* who stands at the center of her own paradise.

Also invoking the Biblical Eve, Judithe Hernández's *Death in the East of Eden* from her *Adam and Eve Series* (2009-2010) depicts a disobedient Eve banished to the Land of Nod (the palm trees in the background signifying East Los Angeles), here shown wearing a crown of deer antlers, her sleeping naked body draped over the hood of a lowrider car. For Hernández, the "car signifies male culture, but [the image also shows] how women have played into

Figure 42. *Death on the East of Eden* by Judithe Hernández © 2009. Used by permission of the artist.

their own subjugation by submitting to the pressure to be good wives and good mothers" (personal communication 2013). For Hernández, the antlers are an ambiguous symbol; they can represent both male power and a female warrior spirit. "There's something wonderfully feminine and yet dangerous about antlers," she adds.

But the antlers aren't the only male symbol that Hernández's Eve wears; rather the antlers are part of a mask reminiscent of Mexican male wrestlers from the popular sport known as Lucha Libre, where the wrestlers traditionally don a mask to hide their identities and create heroic alter egos in the ring. "Masks, masking, and unmasking are themes that pervade not only *lucha libre*, but also Mexican cultural discourse as a whole," writes Heather Levi in *The World of Lucha Libre*. Not only is the mask "a metonym for *lucha libre*, worn by perhaps half to two-thirds of Mexico's wrestlers," but also, it has a signifying function that represents indigenous Mexican national identity. And since *lucha libre* is considered a male sport only, the indigenous Mexican national identity is also male-centric. Indeed, by "connecting *lucha libre* to the indigenous world, the mask is seen as central to the Mexicanization [and machoization] of the genre."[7]

Commenting on what led her to create her *Luchadora Trilogy*, Hernández attributes its genesis to questioning the power of the *luchador*'s mask. "How does its extreme masculinity change when put on a woman?" she wondered (personal communication 2013). Tired of seeing women, and particularly Chicanas, represented as either second-class citizens or victims of their circumstances and life choices, and knowing the lasting impact of religious iconography, Hernández wanted to use crowns of thorns to represent the sacrifices made by women in Chican@/Latin@ culture. From this crown of thorns idea evolved the image of the horned woman, or Devil woman, the artist again evoking a Christian motif. In 2008, she created the middle image of what would become her tryptich—the horned woman now depicted as a naked

Figure 43. *Trilogy* by Judithe Hernández © 2010. Used by permission of the artist.

warrior in an antler mask. This piece was the progenitor of all the *luchadora* images, including those in her *Adam and Eve* series.

Filled with a "crushing sadness," as Hernández describes it, the horned warrior woman's eyes are closed as she centers herself in her internal space, perhaps preparing for battle, weeping tears of blood like the tattoos that gang members wear to signify their prison sentences. At each side of her, we see two representations of, ostensibly, the middle figure's naked back and backside. With her arms outstretched and her hair tied up in a long braid, she strikes a more vulnerable pose, her *luchadora* mask festooned with ribbons and a crown of thorns. Meant to signify the figure's intrinsic femininity, no doubt, the ribbons appear to fly about each woman's head like Medusa snakes. Unlike the more realistic frontal depiction of the middle image, the flesh of the woman's back and buttocks in the outer panels is colored blue and green. "I never want to be accused of exploiting women or objectifying them in any way," explains the artist. "The best way to eliminate or prevent this criticism is by changing the color of the body. The less realistic the image, the less sexualized the interpretation of the female form" (personal communication).[8]

Figure 44. *Sebastiana: Lengua Negra* by Delilah Montoya © 2002. Used by permission of the artist.

A self-denominated *"hocicona,"* or loud-mouth, Delilah Montoya has been depicting warrior women in her photography and mixed media installations for over two decades (see, especially, her work on women boxers). Indeed, her DVD video installation, *San Sebastiana—Ángel de la Muerte* (2001), which appears in the *Saintly Sinners & Sinful Saints* show appropriates the Penitente Brotherhood's[9] legend of San Sebastiana, which itself is an appropriation and resignification of the life of the martyred Saint Sebastian, an early Roman Christian put to death in the second century A.D. under the rule of pagan Emperor Diocletian. Patron saint of archers, athletes, soldiers and holy Christian death, and invoked against the bubonic plague, Saint Sebastian is usually portrayed as a young man in a loincloth strapped to a tree or a pillar, his body pierced with arrows. Saint Sebastian is a popular figure in the art world, with depictions by

Figure 45. *Sebastiana: Ahora* by Delilah Montoya © 2002. Used by permission of the artist.

European masters Botticelli, Titian, El Greco, Rubens and Dalí (among many others). In the Penitente Brotherhood's take on the legend, Saint Sebastian becomes San Sebastiana, the female symbol of death. "Once he crossed the ocean, did this saint cross genders as well?" Montoya asks in her artist's statement.

In the video, which is structured in parallel storylines—one in Doña Sebastiana's perspective and the other in the point of view of God, with whom she is arguing—the sexy Doña Sebastiana is admiring her reflection in the mirror and gossiping about her older neighbor's pregnancy. "Secrets in the barrio circulate faster than money," she says, happy that she never "played with fire" and got pregnant. She doesn't see the repulsive *calaca* that God and Los Hermanos see, but rather a young and sensuous woman with "deep cleavage and big, soft breasts." She is protesting about having to serve God as the angel of death, gathering souls "like a tax collector," a job she feels is beneath her. But God is both poetic and persuasive: "Death is not a period but a comma in the story of life," he says. "Life only exists in the presence of death." Still, Sebastiana will not concede; well she knows that people fear death, and their fear will make them hate and avoid her company. "At least as a puta, people would run *to* me rather than *from* me," Doña Sebastiana says, revealing her own comfort with her "bad girl" reputation and her fearlessness in the presence of the Almighty. Finally, God gives her an offer she cannot refuse, promising that he will canonize her as San Sebastiana in exchange for her saintly service of "seduc[ing] the creation of life," and collecting spent souls "with supple care." She likes the ring of it—*San* Sebastiana rather than Santa Sebastiana, a melding of male and female, good boy and bad girl—and agrees to God's terms. The video ends with her wondering how close she will be to the status of Archangel.

There are two ways to watch the video: by clicking the blue button, we see the sensuous diva that Doña Sebastiana used to be; by clicking the red button, we see the skeletal specter that she has become over the ages. In essence, the tragedy of San Sebastiana is that she cannot see the mask of death that she is sentenced to wear for eternity as God's "handmaiden." Perhaps all she has in common with her namesake is that both were persecuted by their communities and paraded around in a sinner's cart. Unlike her namesake, however, who is the patron saint of holy Christian death, San Sebastiana is the patron of the unholy, particularly the women who have forgotten their place as handmaidens to their lords and masters, their fathers and husbands. To this day in the mountains of New Mexico, secular death is personified as San Sebastiana, and imagined as a *calaca* riding in a cart. She is the northern New Mexican equivalent of the Mexican legend of La Llorona, the Weeping Mother, sentenced to wander the riverbanks for eternity in search for the children she betrayed with her evil ways.

Joining Montoya's wicked angel of death in her sinful sojourn through this exhibition at the Fowler Museum was Alma Lopez's *Queer Santas* and *Juan Soldado*, Liliana Wilson's *Eva*, and Judithe Hernández's *Luchadoras*—all "bad girls" on the rise. Again.

9
MALINCHE'S RIGHTS

I'm not here to apologize. After so many years, even our language has changed. This is what is possible: you won't understand me; or, my words may still be clotted in my throat. But I can't lose heart. As my grandmother used to say: *nunca es tarde cuando la dicha es buena*, it's never too late for good intentions. I've come to bring you prickly pears. Look at them. So fresh. So red. Their juice slides over the letters of your name. Your tombstone needed this touch of blood. Now your nickname, *EL PA-PACITO,* makes more sense.

Father, last night I dreamt you again. In the movie of the dream, the whole family was at a party, a *quinceañera* or a baptism, a fancy initiation of some kind. You were sitting alone at a big table, dressed in tails, a white silk shirt, a pleated sash, a black bow tie. The most handsome man in the room, as usual. You were older than fifty-two. You looked like a grandfather with silver-gray hair and two long furrows on each side of your forehead where your scalp shone like wax. You were leaning back against the wall, eyes closed, and you seemed to be sleeping.

At a table next to yours, my brother was watching you, a look of terror on his face, his green eyes tinged with sadness. I approached your table and squatted beside you, my chin on the tablecloth, watching you closely, like my brother. Suddenly your face moved. A kind of painful grimace, a jerk of your lips, a twitch of your eyes and I jumped and yelled to my brother.

"I know," said my brother. "I think he's alive."

I turned and looked at you again, and again your body moved. Now you stretched like a cat after a long nap. I ran to tell everyone that you were alive, that you were moving, but nobody listened. I returned to your table. On a couch directly in front of you, my sister was breast-feeding her newborn.

Your eyes opened like wounds. You gazed for a while at my sister, then you said, "*Hija*, bring me something to eat!"

My sister ignored you as if she hadn't heard. I felt a great pain knowing you were hungry, you who never ate, who made faces at the steaming dishes of *frijol con puerco*, *chiles rellenos* and *arroz con pollo* that my grandmother would prepare for you to tempt you away from your rum or brandy.

Seeing that my sister didn't respond to your request, you got to your feet and asked for food again, but as soon as you took the first step, your legs collapsed and you fell to the floor. You got up and fell two more times. By the third fall, your body had decomposed. Your clothes had rotted, and your flesh looked like raw meat marbled with worms. Your legs were twisted, your knees to the back and you had no lips left, only those white false teeth.

Some time passed in the dream, but afterward we all returned to that place, which had become an airplane with blue seats. You were sitting at the back of the plane, and I remember clearly hearing you say how hungry you were, but nobody, nobody but me, was listening.

I went to the back and said, "But you're dead."

"Yes," you said, "the bad part is dead, but the good part is alive and hungry."

I ran up and down the plane, yelling to my aunts and uncles what you had said, but it was as though I were speaking to the dead.

I decided to give you something to eat. I took you a carton of milk and some butter cookies wrapped in wax paper. I served you a tall glass of creamy milk. You asked me to join you. I thought to myself that the milk was going to curdle with all the mescal I'd had to drink the night before, but I served myself a glass anyway. When I peeled the paper off one of the cookies, I noticed that the cookie was a host.

Suddenly I wanted to stroke you. You seemed so innocent sitting there with your milk and cookies, like a boy playing at holy communion. I closed my eyes and stroked your stubbly face (you who took such pride in a smooth shave), my cheek against your cheek, but when I opened my eyes, I saw that I was stroking the carton of milk.

Then I heard your voice. You told me to ask everyone on the plane to write something about you or about this situation. I distributed pencils and paper to everyone, and I begged them to do as you said, but nobody wanted to write. We'll be arriving at our destination soon, they said, we don't have time to write. I insulted all of them. I could no longer tolerate their indifference.

"You've always treated him like this," I shouted. "And you still have the nerve to criticize me for not having gone to his funeral. You can all go to hell. I'm going to write. I don't care where we're going or when we're getting there. I won't get off this plane until I finish my letter."

The angle of the camera focused on the paper, and I could clearly make out the words that I was writing, my handwriting that of a nine year-old not yet fluent in cursive. Strangely, the letter was in English.

Dear Dad,

if you want to heal your body, you have to rest a lot and you should hold this crystal pyramid in your right hand so that its energy can go up your arm and heal your body.

Dad, you wrote to me only twice. On my sixth birthday, you sent me a letter telling me not to cut my hair. To obey my grandmother. To use the one dollar check you had enclosed for candy and chocolates. Twenty-one years passed before I received the postcard you sent me from Las Vegas. You promised that now that you knew my address you were going to write more often. I never saw your handwriting again.

My grandmother says you were very bitter about what I had chosen, that "abnormal life," she said, that life without a man. Before me, the one responsible for your cirrhosis was my mother for having left you. Then my brother and sister for treating you *como un cero a la izquierda*, a zero to the left, as if you didn't exist. Then I had to carry the cross. I wonder, Dad, did you ever notice that blame didn't stick to you? It's as if you pollinated us with your blame.

Instead of attending your funeral, I escaped to Mexico, but even there the cold dust of your breath reached me. In Teotihuacan, on the Avenue of the Dead, an indigenous woman was selling crystal amulets in the shape of pyramids. It took me a while to decide, but finally I selected a miniature temple of the sun in green glass, its four sides reflecting the afternoon light. I held it up to the sun in my right hand and felt a rainbow arching through my arm and through my body. I knew this amulet would protect me from you.

Then, in Guanajuato, in the museum of dead bodies mummified by the very stones of the graveyard, bodies with tongues and pubic hair, each one laid out in a glass casket as if to await the kiss of Prince Charming, I stroked the toes of a Chinese mummy. I didn't do it for you. It was not meant to honor your death.

Understand me. I didn't come to the funeral because I didn't want to see you inside a box, surrounded by artificial flowers and tears like some king of the screen. They say you looked very handsome, Papacito, as always. That you wore a white suit and that the coffin was made of a very fine wood. My mother told me that a compadre of yours had brought you a bouquet of gardenias.

"It was a habit of my compadre's," said your compadre, "on the nights we boys went out, to buy a bunch of gardenias from a *viejita* who was always on the corner of la Lerdo and *el Malecón.*"

In Oaxaca, on a night heavy with mescal, my lover and I were sitting at the edge of the main plaza, surrounded by children selling Chiclets and flowers, baskets and shoeshines. We listened to "La Llorona" twice in a row, and then I bought gardenias from the smallest saleswoman in the world.

That night you came to visit me, just as you used to visit me every time I followed in your footsteps and got drunk. But I cast you out. I opened my mouth over the toilet and let you go, a thick and bitter substance that stuck to the bowl like the *atole* of death. It wasn't until the next day that I realized it was the gardenias that had brought you. For that reason, I have never again bought gardenias.

I'm not here to apologize. When my aunt called and told me you had died suddenly of an embolism, while the whole family was at breakfast, I felt a great calm. The clot of words in my throat at last began to loosen, and at last I could let the blood of your memory run free.

That's why I've come to bring you prickly pears, the sacred fruit of Huitzilopochtli. Whether it's a peace offering or another sacrifice, time will tell.

☙ ☙ ☙

When the white man of the hairy face came to Malinal Tenepal's cell, she was praying to Coatlicue, goddess of life and death. Another man in a long black dress and a white collar accompanied the bearded one. He was not a man of her own blood, but his face and hands were the same deep bronze of her own skin. He stared at her with traitor's eyes.

"What do you want?" Malintzin said to the traitor.

He spoke two languages, just as she did, and they had one in common.

"This man wants to know if you are the one they call La Lengua?"

She turned her gaze to the bearded one and saw that he had dark hair climbing up his arms like fur, and his stockinged legs looked scrawny as a chicken's. The symbol of the new god hung over his groin.

She didn't mince words. "Yes, I'm the interpreter. But I'm busy."

The traitor translated her reply. The bearded one tossed his head back and a wild laugh came out of his mouth. His tongue was a pink snake coiled between his teeth.

"How is it you know our language?" she asked the traitor.

"I was a slave of the Maya's for eight years," he said, "until Capitán Hernán Cortés rescued me."

The man named Cortés said something to the traitor.

"He says you have to follow him; he is going to change your ways."

"I told you, I'm busy. Tell him I can't go, I'm praying."

Again, the traitor translated her response.

The bearded one looked at her with sparks of blood in his eyes. He held out his hand to her and said something that the translator didn't bother translating. Was he expecting her to bend her knee to him and kiss his hand?

She laughed and the bearded one pulled his hand back. He exchanged words with the traitor, and then the traitor said, "This man wants to know, where are your rosary and your crucifix? He says you can't pray without these things. He says you are a sinner, you are godless and he has come to save you."

Malintzin began to feel dizzy. An attack of words was coming on, strange words, words that she didn't know, secret words of the goddesses. She didn't want the stranger to hear her chant. That would be a true sin. Her stomach convulsed, and she shot a stream of bitter liquid at the feet of the bearded one. The first syllables were rising. She had to escape. She had to run. Those words could not be heard by any man, white or of her people. She vomited again and a chameleon shot out. The bearded one jumped back, shouting in his strange tongue to the traitor. The chameleon grew and grew, a snake rattle on its coiled tail, rattling its warning in the bearded one's face.

"In the name of the Father, the Son and the Holy Spirit," intoned the traitor, casting on Malintzin drops of acid from a flask he carried around his neck. The chameleon shrunk with each drop.

Little by little the nausea stopped. The effort had exhausted her, but at least she had managed to save the words. She could barely breathe. Her body trembled, and the sweat that dripped from the hair under her arms burned her like the traitor's acid

She felt something fresh against her lips. The bearded one had brought her the water jar beside her altar. She looked at him for a moment before drinking, and with hands of paper, with the traitor's help, she lifted the jar and let the water of Tonantzin's well wash her inside and out. The traitor seemed to know what she wanted, for he lifted the jar to let the water flow through her hair and down her forehead. The bearded one said something to the traitor and the traitor translated.

"He says you are baptized now. Your Christian name is Marina. Tomorrow he will come to take you to matins."

Malinche did not respond, just lowered her head in a gesture of acceptance. A cacophony of rattles filled her ears and her temples started to throb with a shooting pain.

That night, Malinal prepared herself well. With the help of her sister slaves whom their cacique was going to present to the bearded one as tribute for vanquishing the Tlaxcalans and other enemies, she rubbed the walls of her sex with the thorny skin of some prickly pears. She left the skins inside, and the red juice of the fruit spilled down her legs. Afterward, she decorated her hair with peacock plumes and lay down on her *petate* to await her fate.

The bearded one arrived with the first rooster's crow. Upon seeing that she bled, he felt his milk boil and he barely had time to pull down his hose. When he found himself inside that swollen space, that nest of thorns, where his member had gotten trapped like a snake, his screams bubbled with his seed.

Never had Doña Marina felt so much in control of her own destiny.

ᘓᑧᕉ ᘓᑧᕉ ᘓᑧᕉ

Do you remember, Dad, the time you came home at dawn and tried to force my mother? I was three years old. I slept on a cot at the foot of your bed. It scared me when you spit that word at her: *¡Cabrona!* And later you stood over my cot and tucked me in.

What about the time I saw you urinating through the bathroom window? You knew I was there. You even played with your *pirulí.* I confess. One night in my grandmother's house I heard you panting, the same sound my boyfriend used to make when I masturbated him in the car.

When the bearded one poked at the skirts of La Malinche, she already knew what to expect. Her mother had explained it to her the night before she sold her to the Mayan traders.

"I'm sorry, Malinalli," her mother had said, "but your stepfather wants his son to be my heir, he wants to kill you, but I said I would get rid of you myself. That's why I'm selling you to these merchants."

"Will I have nothing, then, Mother?"

"You will have your wits and your tongue," her mother said. "Your body will not belong to you, nor will the children you bring into this world. But your wits and your tongue will be your salvation."

How did her mother know she would be traded among men? From the Mayans to the Tabascans to the Spaniards. What happened with the bearded one was nothing more than another tribute to another conquistador. Some hairless and heathen, others bearded and baptized in the new faith.

My grandmother always accused me of being a heathen. She used to say I was going to roast in hell because I never prayed the rosary and because I chewed on the host without having gone to confession. What she didn't know is that you, Our Father who art in heaven, took me to the matinee every Saturday and lifted my skirt and fed me our daily bread.

Unlike you, my boyfriend was a gringo and had a beard, but he also liked doing it at the movies. What happened with that bearded one was nothing more than another tribute to another conquistador.

And now, enough of all this false homage. These prickly pears are the rights you violated, the secret words I had to swallow.

I'm soaked to the marrow. A downpour has just flooded the desert. The rain has washed away the blood of the cactus that tainted your name. Your stone is clean now. *EL PAPACITO* fresh as the cemetery grass. The rattles I hear are my own teeth.

10

THE CODEX NEPANTLA PROJECT: TRANSINTERPRETATION AS POCHA POETICS, POLITICS AND PRAXIS

Chicana feminists have been publishing their scholarship and theories of resistance and social change since the 1970s, and yet, their work is not broadly available in Spanish translation. Spanish-speaking Mexican and Latin American feminists, particularly at the grassroots level, have no access to Chicana feminist/lesbian epistemology, and no knowledge of the counter-hegemonic ideas and concepts that Chicana feminists have been constructing and using to analyze, challenge and revolutionize the structures of power and inequalities that are based in race, class, sex, gender, culture and language oppression, otherwise known as patriarchy—an ideology that dominates most of the world, but that in the United States is especially virulent for Chicana-identified activists and scholars whose identities straddle the US-Mexico border. It is this binational and bilingual problem that the Codex Nepantla Project seeks to address.

The idea for the Codex Nepantla Project came to me in Mexico City in 2011 at the Tercera Semana de Cultura Lésbica Feminista LesVoz, a festival of Lesbian Feminist Culture sponsored by LesVoz,[1] the oldest grassroots lesbian feminist organization in Mexico. As with other LesVoz events, programming for the festival featured the cultural production of Mexican and Chicana lesbians, including readings, performances and a group art exhibition. My wife, Alma Lopez and I were invited to speak at Semana Lésbica about our lesbian feminist activism in Los Angeles. Alma spoke on our recently published co-edited book, *Our Lady of Controversy* about the censorship controversy that took place in Santa Fe, New Mexico in 2001 over her small photo-collage, *Our Lady*, which depicts a representation of the Virgin of Guadalupe dressed in nothing but flowers. Alma shared her revolutionary interpretation of this revered cultural icon. I presented on my research on the Juárez femicides and the transhistorical frame of the "bad woman" by which the victims of these heinous crimes were framed and judged.

At the close of the event, Mariana Pérez Ocaña, one of the founders of LesVoz, invited us to attend the afternoon session of the *Mini Encuentro Nacional de Lesbianas Feministas*. Because it was a closed-to-the-public retreat of lesbian feminist organizations in Mexico with whom LesVoz wanted to create a network, or *red de organizaciones lesbofeministas de México*,[2] there were representatives from ten or eleven groups from other parts of Mexico in attendance. After establishing the ground rules for the gathering—one of which was that Alma and I were there merely as listeners, not participants in the discussion—we heard a riveting presentation on the history of Mexican feminism by activist Yan María Yaloltl Castro that ended with a strong critique of how "*lo cuir*" (or Eurocentric male queer theory)[3] was cannibalizing the academic feminists at the National Autonomous University of Mexico (UNAM), while the burgeoning trans movement, led in Mexico by transwomen who did not support the work of lesbian organizations like LesVoz, was colonizing lesbian feminism in the community. A discussion ensued between those who wanted to open the network and their organizations to queers and trans folk and those who adamantly wanted to keep the integrity of a separatist lesbian network—a fundamental political and philosophical difference that Chicana lesbian/feminists had also been grappling with in our national associations, NACCS and MALCS[4] since the turn of the 21st century. Ultimately, this difference would prevent the development of a national network of lesbian feminist organizations in Mexico, but that afternoon, it was the first time all these lesbian feminist groups had come together to discuss the possibility of forming a cohesive front united in the same struggle for lesbian survival and representation.

I found the raw discussion both fascinating and frustrating. I was fascinated because Alma and I were witnessing a historic gathering of lesbian organizations in Mexico and frustrated that I could not join the conversation. So instead of speaking, I listened and scribbled furiously what I wanted so badly to say. *Chicana feminists have gone through this,* I wrote, *and so many have written about similar fundamental differences that have divided the Chicano Movement and Chicana feminism as well.* Noticing that I had something to contribute, Mariana asked the group if anybody would mind if the Chicana *compañeras* addressed the gathering. Politely, they gave me the floor, and I thanked them for acknowledging me and for allowing us to be in the room. I talked about sexism within Chicanismo and racism within Anglo feminism and homophobia within both, and how Chicana lesbians wrote about those struggles from the margins of our mutually exclusive communities, and how they had invented *teorías* like *la facultad* and *la nueva mestiza* (Gloria Anzaldúa 1987), *sitios y lenguas* and the decolonial imaginary (Emma Pérez 1991 and 1999), and differential/oppositional consciousness/*conciencia diferencial/oposicional* (Chela Sandoval 2000) to help us analyze our differences and name the sources of our (dis)empowerment. I related the way Gloria Anzaldúa and Cherríe Moraga had appropriated Mexican icons Malinche, Coatlicue and Coyolxauhqui to embody the psychic and physical violence we had all felt within Chicano patriarchy for our supposed betrayal of our *familias*, whether at home or among our *carnales*/brothers in the Chicano revolution.

I concluded my remarks with an example. At the 2005 meeting of the National Association for Chicana and Chicano Studies
in Miami, Florida, a majority of the Lesbian Caucus, composed
of a younger generation that preferred the queer label, sexual flu-
idity and nonbinary gender identification, voted in favor of
changing the name of the caucus to the Lesbians, BiMujeres and
Trans Caucus, after more than twenty years of being a woman-
only, lesbian-only safe space—a space and recognition in the association that the Chicana lesbians who had founded the Lesbian
Caucus back in 1990 had fought bitterly to get after years of sexist and homophobic treatment within the association.[5]

Except for the women of LesVoz, the others had never heard
of Chicana feminism. Some of them had heard of Chicanas, others had not. Of course, they had all read or at least heard of Anglo
and French feminists Judith Butler, Lillian Faderman, Adrienne
Rich, Simone de Beauvoir, and Monique Wittig; but these radical grassroots gender and sexuality Mexican activists were not
familiar with the names of our most radical and prolific Chicana
lesbian scholar-activists, much less the early organizers of the
Chicana feminist movement. Nor did they really get the concept
of Chicana feminism as a separate theoretical discourse from
mainstream American feminism. In fact, some of the attendees
thought Alma and I were "*gringa*" feminists, maybe because I
am light-skinned and we live in Los Angeles, or maybe because
we spoke to each other in English, and they could hear the
pochismo in our Spanish, the hybrid language of the border. In
any case, they saw us at outsiders.

After the meeting ended, we invited everyone to come to our
talk at the UNAM. Marisa Belausteguigoitia, then Director of the
Programa Universitario de Estudios de Género (PUEG) and a pi-
oneer in the use of Anzalduan pedagogy in the Mexican public
university classroom, had asked us to present some of our work
to her graduate class. Little did we realize that the political breach
between feminist academics and working-class *lesbofeministas*

(their preferred label) is particularly wide in Mexico, and that, although the UNAM has a program on gender and feminist studies, there is very little outreach to or integration of community organizations that serve the same interests. As community activists, organizers and laborers, *las compañeras* of these lesbian organizations did not feel welcome at the university and could not see themselves occupying any space at the PUEG.

"We won't feel comfortable," Mariana explained. "And besides, *las compañeras* don't understand English."

In a nutshell, that was the issue. Grassroots Mexican feminists and *lesbofeministas* did not read Chicana theory, not so much because our work was considered more *gringa* than Mexican and more academic than activist, but simply because our work is not available in Spanish translation. While they could read Anglo-American and French feminist writing in Spanish, our Spanish-only grassroots *compañeras* had (and continue to have) little access to Chicana feminist theory and Chicana lesbian feminist *conocimiento* because our work has not been translated. That was a huge discovery for me, a problem which (I naively imagined) had an easy solution.

On the flight back to Los Angeles, I wrote page after page of questions in my journal. How does the Chicana lesbian/feminist fight for equality, representation and recognition in both the Chicano Movement and the white Feminist Movement mirror the exclusionary experiences of working-class *lesbofeminista activistas* in Mexico? Why are Anglo-American and French feminist publications translated into Spanish in Mexico, but not the work of Chicana lesbian/feminists with whom, ostensibly, our Mexican counterparts have more in common? Is it only a linguistic issue, or are there ideological and historical reasons that keep Chicana lesbian/feminist knowledge inaccessible to a Spanish-speaking audience? Do Chicanas write predominantly in English because we hate Spanish or because we are *pochas*, academically educated in the United States? To what degree does Octavio Paz's judgement on Chicanos, or *pachucos*, as lost and lonely Mexicans, "sinister clown[s] whose purpose is to cause terror instead of laughter" (Paz, *Labyrinth* 16) continue to inform the Mexican imaginary of who or what the Chicanx community actually is? Do Mexicans continue to see us as "traitors" to our Mexican culture for "forgetting" our Spanish? Do Mexicans realize that growing up in the monolingual United States took away our choice to learn Spanish, let alone use it in a way that was linguistically or grammatically correct? What do Chicana lesbian/feminist theorists and writers contribute intellectually and politically to the discourse of gender and sexuality in colonial patriarchy, as well as to national constructions of *mexicanidad* or *americanidad*?

As the artist in the family, Alma added a visual component to my theoretical ruminations: how would seeing what Chicana artists have done with Mexican legends and iconography help to open up the borders of communication between us? Chicana artists have been creating a visual language of Chicana lesbian/feminist empowerment using revised representations of Mexican iconography since the 1970s. *Malinche, Coatlicue, Sor Juana, la Soldadera, la Catrina, la Sirena, la Virgen de Guadalupe*—all are popular Mexican icons that have been carried across the border, recoded and transinterpreted for a new audience of US-born and/or -bred Mexicans and Latinx people to assert a cultural pride and specificity not tied to a linguistic identity.

By the summer of 2011, the Latina/o Studies library of scholarly and literary texts (in English, of course) had grown exponentially, and titles by queers and women of color were the most prolific. Individual Chicana/Latina feminist critical interventions virtually exploded in the fields of art, art history, cultural studies, education, gender studies, history, linguistics, literary criticism, media studies, public policy, queer studies, sociology, urban planning. Transformative Chicana lesbian/feminist anthologies started to populate the tables of university presses at academic conferences, and we also saw an increase in Chicana- and Chicano-authored novels, young adult books and memoirs published by both mainstream and independent presses.[6] Indeed, mega-publishing houses started imprints that marketed directly to a Latinx audience, and some published original works in Spanish as well as English. It was as if the book industry of the United States were suddenly discovering that Latinos/as were not only quickly becoming the largest minority in the nation, but also, that they were a book-buying culture. The same cannot be said of the publishing industry in Mexico, which for the most part has ignored the publishing prowess of its American diaspora, particularly the work authored by Chicanas.[7]

The great Mexicana writer, Elena Poniatowska herself had spoken to the issue of Chicana ostracism on both sides of the border twenty years earlier in a lecture she delivered at Hampshire College, published five years later in the academic journal *MELUS* and titled simply, "Chicanas and Mexicanas." Poniatowska stated,

> Chicanos are caught between two worlds that reject them: Mexicans who consider them traitors, and Americans who want them only as cheap labor. . . . Even now, very few Mexican writers care for Chicano writers and poets, and even fewer women writers take Chicana writers into account. . . . Chicanos with American passports are still considered aliens, and women especially are seen as continuing the tradition of La Malinche, the ultimate traitor. [. . .] To be a Chicano is not easy, but to be a Chicana is even harder. To be a writer in Mexico is not easy, but to be a woman writer sometimes makes no sense at all. A Chicana writer in the United States gets the worst of both conditions: being a woman and a Chicana aspiring to become a writer. . . . In Mexico, the work of Chicano writers like Tomás Rivera, Tino Villanueva, Rudolfo Anaya, Miguel Méndez has been published, but no Chicana can make the same claim.[8]

Clearly, the time was more than ripe for showing that Chicana lesbian/feminist knowledge was its own intellectual and political movement with more than forty years of textual discourse which not only deserved but needed to be read by our sisters south of the border. Because we share a common cultural root and a colonial experience based on race, class, gender, and sexual oppression in a world order ruled by the laws of the straight, white, rich, Father; because we fight a common struggle against decolonization, misogyny, and homophobia; and because we have developed a repertoire of radical theories and methods of self-empowerment and solidarity to help us navigate our bifurcated lives in the midst of a xenophobic patriarchy, we have authorized ourselves to write our own *autohistorias* and *autohistoria-teorías*,[9] as Anzaldúa calls them, instead of waiting for somebody else to write or theorize our stories for us. And so, the seed for the idea that became the Codex Nepantla Project found fertile soil.

Our Mission, Should We Decide to Accept It

We returned from that Mexico City trip in 2011 inspired by the idea of translating Chicana feminist and Chicana lesbian feminist theory into Spanish and visual art and making these translations freely accessible to grassroots activists via the worldwide web. We saw it as a Chicana Lesbian/Feminist Codex, and Alma created a blog called Codex Nepantla (see www.codexnepantla. blogspot.com). I wrote out a Mission Statement[10] and we invited twenty academic colleagues (many of whom are the very scholars and writers whose work we aimed to translate), students and ABDs, as well as Chicana/x and Latina/x and lesbian/queer visual artists to join us in forming a team of theoretical border crossers, or linguistic/artistic *nepantleras*,[11] who would translate Chicana lesbian/feminist theory into Spanish and visual art, facilitating access to this critical, oppositional, counter-hegemonic discourse for Spanish-speaking grassroots activists south of the border.

All of the Chicana academics I contacted expressed solidarity with the project. Some admitted to having issues with their own "bad Spanish." Others apologized for not speaking or even reading Spanish. I reassured them that *pocha* poetics was a legitimate form of writing, and that we would use whatever tools we had at our disposal to carry Chicana lesbian/feminist thought across the border on the bridges of our *"sitios y lenguas,"* to cite Emma Pérez. Alma invited other visual artists to help her with the artistic interpretations. Nearly everyone agreed to join the Codex Nepantla Collective, and I received enthusiastic commitments from several graduate students who wanted to participate in the collective as well. We gave all the participants access to the Codex Nepantla Blog site, posted some initial thoughts and waited for people to engage in the dialogue.

Unfortunately, the project stalled almost immediately, as the Codex Nepantla Blog shows, but not for lack of interest. Although the members of the collective were excited by the prospect of doing this scholar-activist work, we soon realized that the task at hand was not only challenging linguistically (as very few of us had any formal training in Spanish or an academic background in translation), but actually daunting ideologically because of all the layers of social anxiety and linguistic terrorism had to be sorted out by each of us individually as well as by the Collective before any translation work was even possible.[12]

The *Pocha* Poetics Seminar

After two years of waiting for any activity (beyond Alma's and mine) on the Codex Nepantla Blog, I realized that the only way to make any progress on this project was to gather everyone together under the same roof for a translation retreat. To that end, I secured a University of California Humanities Research Institute Seminar Grant for a seminar that I called "*Pocha* Poetics in the Translation of Chicana Feminist Theory" that brought together eight faculty and nine graduate students from three UC campuses,[13] as well as from other colleges in Los Angeles and beyond. Hosted by the LGBTQ Studies Program at UCLA (of which I was then chair), the two-day seminar took place in April, 2014, and the main purpose of the gathering was to come together to discuss the feasibility of co-creating this resource, to read essays about the ethics and politics of translation and about translation as a postcolonial process. Most importantly, I wanted all of us to be in the same room to share/theorize/freewrite about our very real apprehensions about translating our own or anybody else's work into Spanish.

I had compiled a massive *Pocha* Poetics Reader for the seminar and invited the faculty to volunteer as discussion leaders for each section. The highly theoretical discussion of the readings quickly narrowed down to practicalities of the process. How do we translate ourselves, especially if we don't speak or write in Spanish? What do we gain by making our work accessible in Spanish? What do we lose by keeping it inaccessible? How do we negotiate the binational shaming and harassment that Chicanas/os receive from both sides of the border for the way we speak: our Mexican-accented Spanish that underscores our "foreignness" in the United States; or, conversely, our English-accented and *pocho* (polluted/degenerate/embarrassing) Spanish that marks our supposed betrayal of our Mexican homeland? How do Chicanas give agency to our own colonized *pocha* tongues in the face of anti-Mexican, anti-immigrant rhetoric north of the border, and anti-*vendida* (sellout), anti-*pocha* dogma south of the Rio Grande? What, in fact, is "*pocha* poetics," and how can we spread this aesthetic on a grassroots scale in Mexico? How does art, and specifically popular and indigenous iconography, function as both a common and a foreign language between Chicanas and Mexicanas? What were we going to call this translation method, anyway?

Those in attendance at the seminar confirmed that they wrote almost exclusively in English. Since none of them were in the field of Spanish Literature, they did not write or publish academic work in Spanish for at least three reasons: a) because they had gone to English-only schools in the United States, b) because they were in academic departments in the United States that required publications in English and c) because of a linguistic incapacity, meaning they never learned to read or write "correctly" in Spanish, even if they could still speak the language with their families. On a deeper level, they feared being thought of as stupid, assimilated, cultural defectors with nothing of value or importance to contribute to "real" Mexicans. In short, they were describing some of the side effects of linguistic terrorism and a deeply internalized colonized tongue. On the second day of the seminar, Alma led us through a stenciling workshop where she taught us how to stencil a word or an image that was important to us and that somehow represented the work we had done at the seminar. She had already created some stencils ahead of time, and one of them was the word POCHA, which several of us decided to screen onto the T-shirts we had brought for the workshop. This alone was empowering, as it helped us to re-signify a word that for too long had been used to demean us. Yes, I'm a *pocha*, not a Mexican, not an American, but both, and neither. *¿Y qué?*

Figure 46. *Pocha* stencil from the *Pocha* Poetics Seminar, April 2014. Photo by the author.

Thick Translation and the Nepantla Paradigm

The only way for Spanish-only grassroots activists to learn about Chicana lesbian/ feminist theory, knowledge and scholarship is for the work to be translated. But translation is not just a matter of changing linguistic codes or substituting content from one language for another. In "The Task of the Translator," Walter Benjamin reminds us that "no translation would be possible if in its ultimate essence it strove for likeness to the original."[14] Literal likeness or equivalency is just the surface of the translator's task; to fully render the many meanings of any translated text, the translator must have a "deeper interpretation" (Benjamin 79) and be able to communicate the text's intentions and connotations, so that the translation "produces in it the echo of the original" (Benjamin 76).

For Kwame Anthony Appiah, translation is not just "an attempt to find ways of saying in one language something that means the same as what has been said in another."[15] The translator must also comprehend the historical, political and cultural contexts of both the text and the author. "[A] translation that draws on and creates that sort of understanding, meets the need to challenge ourselves and our students to go further, to undertake the harder project of a *genuinely informed respect for others*" (Appiah, 817, emphasis added). Thus, to truly translate Chicana lesbian/feminist theory, the translator must have the capacity to effect this "deeper interpretation" that Benjamin expected of the words and sentences on the page. They must have knowledge of the intersectional identity politics that trouble our genders and relationships; awareness of how Chicana theorists appropriate and re-signify Mexican and indigenous icons, legends and cosmographies in the elaboration of that theory; must know that Chicano/a identity is situated in US-Mexican territorial and ideological conflict since the end of the US-Mexico War in 1848. The translator must understand that since the signing of the Treaty of Guadalupe-

Hidalgo, US Mexicans and their Chicana/o descendants have lived in a perpetual Nepantla, in which we are neither *de aquí* (from here) nor *de allá* (from there), but from what Gloria Anzaldúa calls a third culture, which lives in between *el río Bravo* and the Rio Grande—the same river with the same contested history but with different names. This third culture spawns from the wound that forms when the two worlds, countries and cultures "rub against each other and bleed" (*Borderlands* 3). Rather than a marginal location on the fringes of the developed world, as the word *frontier* in English suggests, our *frontera* is Nepantla, the place in the middle, which is what Anzaldúa calls the borderlands, as she explains in one of her interviews:

> With the Nepantla paradigm I try to theorize unarticulated dimensions of the experience of mestizas living in between overlapping and layered spaces of different cultures and social and geographic locations, of events and realities. . . . I see the mestiza as a geography of selves—of different bordering countries—who stands at the threshold of two or more worlds and negotiates the cracks between worlds (268).[16]

In discussing these issues at the *Pocha* Poetics seminar, and the role that bilingualism and biculturality have played in our (post)/(neo)/(de) colonial subjectivities and discourses, we were, I now realize, not only thickly describing (a-la-Clifford Geertz) the intersectionalities and contradictions of Chicana lesbian/feminist ontology and epistemology, but also engaging in what Appiah calls "thick translation," or rather, a "translation that seeks with its annotations and its accompanying glosses to locate the text in a rich cultural and linguistic context" (Appiah 817). For Clifford Geertz,[17] effective ethnography or cultural analysis of the Other must be a "thick description" that integrates layers of data, including social, political, historical, economic, linguistic, religious and other contextual information of the group/people/culture under study. Thus, we could say that, like thick description, Appiah's "thick translation" involves knowing more layers of meaning and interpretation than just linguistic equivalencies.

These layers of interpretation could explain why, in fact, some things are not translatable word for word, as the intentions, assumptions and connotations of some utterances remain knowable only to those who share the cultural codes that would render something legible or intelligible in another code. For the culturally fraught process of bridging the differences between Chicanas and Mexicanas—the former a colonized identity with a history of second- and third-class citizenship within an English-speaking country located in the economic First World, the latter located in the economic Third-World nation-state of a neocolonial Mexico, with a five-hundred-year history of *mestizaje*—the notion of "respect" is critical. But respect is predicated on understanding, the lack of which largely explains why Chicana lesbian/feminist theory (and literature) is not translated or read in Mexico outside of a few university courses. Without accounting for some, if not all, of these layers of interpretation, textual translations are incomplete. To truly translate any text from one meaning system to another, translators must practice thick translation.

Translation theorist Lawrence Venuti argues in his chapter on "Invisibility,"[18] that a "good translation"—one that falls under what he calls "the regime of fluency"—renders the translator invisible. "The more fluent the translation, the more invisible the translator. . . . The translator's invisibility is thus a weird self-annihilation" (Venuti 1, 7). By rendering the text as close to the original as possible, the work of the translation recedes under the fluency of the translator in the other language. Can Chicanas be invisible translators of their own or one another's texts? Or, because we do not, in fact, operate under a "regime of fluency" in Spanish, thanks to a colonized tongue that was never considered fluent enough (read: articulate, eloquent and free of accents) in either English or Spanish, do Chicanas consider ourselves capable of translating texts in our dual mother-tongue? Does our *pochismo*, or code-switching tendency, make us hyper-visible and therefore inimical to the translator's task? As Venuti asserts, "translation wields enormous power in the construction of identities for foreign cultures, and hence, it potentially figures in ethnic discrimination, geopolitical confrontations, colonialism, terrorism [and] war" (Venuti 14).

By producing what I call "translations in the flesh," that is, translations of our own work or the work of other Chicanas with whom we share a knowledge of not only culture, history and language, but also a knowledge of the body and the body's desire, could we not circumvent the "violence of translation" (Venuti 13), the erasure of the translator and/or the negative judgment of our Spanish-writing abilities? Perhaps in this way, Chicana lesbian/feminist writers and their translated texts could actually bridge the differences between Mexican academics and activists, as well as between the academy and the community? Perhaps, as Venuti claims, our translations could "be studied and practiced as *a locus of difference*, instead of the homogeneity that widely characterizes [translation] today?" (Venuti 34). His "locus of difference," like Appiah's "thick translation," is the translator's sign of profound respect for the original author's language, culture, identity and history, and most of all, for the author's embodied knowledge and experience.

Why Chicanas Don't Write in Spanish

For many Chicana academics raised north of the border, Spanish may have been our native or mother tongue, or the spoken language of home and family, or a foreign language that we were trained to forget while growing up and attending English-only schools in the monolingual United States, learning to read, write and speak in "good" English. Some of us precede Bilingual Education, and those who received any formal training in Spanish got it either in grade school or high school, or not until we reached college. In any case, our Spanish vocabulary is limited, and many of us feel ill-equipped to articulate complex intellectual discourse in Spanish. Although we continue to speak some form of Spanish (or Spanglish) with our families, we remain unfamiliar with and intimidated by formal, academic Spanish.

In Mexico, our lack of Spanish fluency is misunderstood (at best), sometimes ridiculed and even shamed. For my Mexican grandparents and their immigrant offspring, the worst insult I could inflict on the family was to "lose my Spanish," which meant forget my Spanish entirely, or, worse, become a *pocha* and speak in both languages at once. This is what "educated" Mexicans call "polluting" or "corrupting" our native language, i.e., Spanish, which is the clearest manifestation of our selling out (in their eyes) and their disrespect (in our eyes). For Mexicans born and raised south of the border, Chicanos are considered traitors to their people and their culture because we are perceived to have willingly turned our back on Mexico and willfully forgotten or abandoned our ancestral language.

In "The Pachuco and Other Extremes," Octavio Paz wrote about living in Los Angeles in the early 1940s and encountering what he perceived to be a different sort of Mexican, the kind "for whom the fact that they are Mexicans is a truly vital problem" (*Labyrinth* 12). These Mexicans, he surmised from watching them in the streets, "feel ashamed of their origin; yet no one would mistake them for authentic North Americans" (*Labyrinth* 13), assumptively because of their phenotypes. Paz found these shame-filled Mexicans "furtive" and "restless," as though they were "wearing disguises, [and were] afraid of a stranger's look because it could strip them and leave them stark naked" (*Labyrinth* 13). This is an interesting choice of words, given that this period of Los Angeles history is during the Zoot Suit Riots, when zoot-suit-wearing Pachucos were, indeed, being targeted for their supposed un-Americanness, and were beaten and stripped on the streets by American civilians and servicemen, then arrested for inciting the riots. Sadly, Paz's perceptions of Pachucos of the 1940s articulate the basis of the Mexican (mis)understanding of Chicano/a identity. For the Pazian mind, Pachucos are Mexican-origin gangs and intransigent rebels caught in an American world that rejects them even as they reject their own native culture and language. Rather than trying to assimilate, Pachucos flaunt their differences, which only enhances their untranslatability in the United States.

> The *pachuco* does not want to become a Mexican again; at the same time, he does not want to blend into the life of North America. His whole being is sheer negative impulse, a tangle of contradictions, an enigma. . . . Whether we like it or not, these persons are Mexicans, are one of the extremes at which the Mexican can arrive. (*Laybrinth* 13-14)

Educated Mexicans like Paz have no knowledge of the contentious racial and cultural history and politics that Mexican-descended Americans have had to endure since the signing of the Treaty of Guadalupe-Hidalgo in 1848. They know that the Gringo invaded Mexico and stole half of Mexico's territory after winning the US-Mexico War, but they have not experienced what it means to grow up in a country that preaches assimilation but practices alienation of anyone whose color, culture and language does not conform to the dominating culture, anyone who fits the description of an "illegal," whether US-born or not. Chicanas/os/xs cannot help but feel a split in their subjectivity, which is composed of two opposing processes, identification and perception—the many ways we see or identify ourselves, and the ways we are perceived by others. And this discrepancy is not limited to life in *el Norte*. During the Chicano Movement of the 1960s-70s, Chicano/a ac-

tivists learned that for all their folkloric *danzas* and political re-
claiming of Mexican indigeneity, educated Mexicans like Octavio
Paz saw them only as foreigners, *vendidos* and cultural clowns,
and thus rejected their claim to a Mexican identity. I argue that it
is because of this deep-seated contempt of US Mexicans that the
corpus of Chicana/o literature and scholarship is not respected,
translated, read, studied or taught in Mexico. Hence, it is up to us
to translate, interpret and teach about ourselves to Mexicanas/os
and other Spanish-only speakers.

Coyotaje Culturolingüístico

In the course of my research on the lack of Chicana feminist
discourse in Spanish, I learned that Chicana writings are, in fact,
not entirely absent from the Mexican consciousness; Chicana literature and theory have entered the Mexican academy at the National Autonomous University of Mexico (UNAM) largely
through the efforts of Professor Claire Joysmith in the Centro de
Investigaciones Sobre América del Norte (CISAN), and Professor Marisa Belausteguigoitia, professor of Pedagogy and former
director of the Programa Universitario de Estudios de Género
(PUEG). Indeed, both scholars have presented conference papers
and published articles, anthologies and monographs that explore
the translation and application of Chicana discourse in Spanish.
Nor has their involvement been strictly textual. In 1993, Professor Joysmith organized a binational *encuentro* between Chicana
and Mexicana writers that led to one of the earliest volumes on
this subject in Mexico. Because of the cultural and linguistic mis-
understandings, the class-based hostilities and gendered ani-
mosities unleashed at that encounter, however, another summit
of this type has not taken place in either Mexico or the United
States. Individual Chicana authors, such as Norma Alarcón,
Norma Cantú and yours truly, have been invited to do talks and
presentations at the UNAM, but the issues raised at the 1993 *en-*

cuentro are never spoken about, nor are we invited to collaborate on the PUEG's translations of Chicana feminist work.[19]

Belausteguigoitia and Joysmith have been studying Chicana feminist theory and Chicana literary interventions (respectively) for decades. For Joysmith, Chicana writers are linguistic Malinches, not traitors but translators of life in-between Mexico and the United States, life in Nepantla, who have appropriated the language of the Anglo colonizer to subvert and, as Norma Klàhn says, "indict the long history of oppression and defacement of a language and a culture,"[20] which are the colonizing tactics of all empires.

In 2012, Joysmith published an anthology of testimonial Chicana poetry in Spanish, titled *Cantar de espejos: poesía testimonial chicana de mujeres,* for which she served as editor, translator and literary *coyote* in reverse, engaged in the surreptitious labor of crossing Chicana literature into the Mexican mainstream. I want to pay particular attention to Joysmith's introductory remarks regarding the complexities involved in bringing the bi-coded linguistic ruptures and differential textualities of Chicana poetics and *pochismo* to a Mexican audience that not only does not understand but actually holds in contempt the way Chicanas/os speak (or don't speak, the way we "butcher") Spanish. Indeed, Joysmith sees this collection of translated Chicana poetry as a *"coyotaje culturolinguístico de las chicanididades femeninas . . . desde el 'otro lado' hacia 'este lado,'"*[21] in other words, "as a cultural-linguistic illegal crossing in reverse of Chicana writings . . . from the other side to this side." The "singing mirrors" in her title evoke the "smoking mirrors" through which the oracles of the ancient empire of the Mexicas/Aztecs foretold the demise of the Quinto Sol/Fifth Sun, ruled by the War God Huitzilopochtli. It would be during the Quinto Sol that the indigenous inhabitants of Mexico would experience the racial/cultural/spiritual European conquest that would result in the birth of a new race, the mestizo race of the Americas. In essence, Chicanas represent the Anzaldúan "new mestizas" in which Mexicans can see themselves reflected, who have transformed their colonized mother tongue into a hybrid poetry and song. It was the "*coyotaje culturolinguístico*," or the "illegal" cultural/linguistic crossing of Chicana writers from the US to Mexico that most caught my eye, for that is exactly the subversive action proposed by the Codex Nepantla project.

While directing the PUEG, Belausteguigoitia—whose Ph.D. is in Ethnic Studies from UC Berkeley—was already teaching a course on Chicana Theory and Discourse at the UNAM. Under her leadership, the program initiated a colloquium series called "*Güeras y Prietas*," in honor of Gloria Anzaldúa, held every October 12, as a counter-narrative on race, gender, sexuality and class celebrated on the traditional Día de la Raza, or Columbus Day. Moreover, Belausteguigoitia has served as advisor to Chicana/o Studies Ph.D. students from the University of California at Santa Barbara, and with her former PUEG graduate advisee, Coco Magallanes (both members of Codex Nepantla), Belausteguigoitia has co-authored several articles on the work of Gloria Anzaldúa, Chela Sandoval and Norma Alarcón. In their articles, they focus on how this body of knowledge (marginalized or ignored in Mexico, but embraced in Spain) can be used to open pedagogical borders that in many ways bring Mexicans back to their indigenous roots. Indeed, in their entry in the *Routledge Companion to Latino/a Literature*, titled "Chicana/o and Latina/o Literary Studies in Mexico," Belausteguigoitia and Magallanes assert that Chicana feminist discourses can be "framed as pedagogies of decolonization . . . [that help] our students understand and articulate experiences of lived discrimination based on vectors of difference such as race, sexuality, gender, and class."[22] These critical teaching and learning strategies connect Mexican students with "the *other* in ourselves; in a sense, Chicanas/os for Mexicans are a perfect example of being *others* and *selves* at the same time" (Belausteguigoitia and Magallanes 97).

Referring to these radical classroom maneuvers as "pedagogies of the double," that pair Chicana/o writers with Mexican counterparts (such as pairing Anzaldúa with Octavio Paz!), Belausteguigoitia and Magallanes show how this doubling or mirroring allows Mexican students to find their voices as political subjects of a colonial experience that they now have the language (i.e., Chicana feminist theory) to deconstruct and by which to "return home" to their cultural *mestizaje* and indigenous roots. Besides illustrating the difference between the colonial, the decolonial and the postcolonial, their pedagogy shows how Chicana feminist and Chicano nationalist ideologies have appropriated Mexican indigenous discourses, myths and resistance strategies in the formation of their decolonizing epistemologies. In short, Mexican students at the UNAM learn about the resistant methodologies of their indigenous past through Anzaldúa's Chicana feminist theory.

As a pedagogical tool, Anzaldúan theory finds purchase in the working-class Mexican student's psyche. But how, exactly, is this Anzaldúan theory translated? How are Mexican students learning about the intersectional oppressions that Chicanas continue to face in our own families, communities, universities and professional lives? Are they, in fact, learning any Chicano/a history, going back to the Treaty of Guadalupe-Hidalgo in 1848, to understand the consequences of territorial displacement, the generations of second-class citizenship, the daily battles with linguistic and cultural incommensurabilities that exist between US-Mexicans and US Americans? Without this historical context, I argue, it is not fully possible for Chicana feminist theories to be studied, interpreted and implemented as part of a decolonizing pedagogical process in Mexico. What might be missing in the Mexican interpretation of Gloria Anzaldúa's "Coyolxauhqui Imperative" and "Coatlicue State"? How would UC Riverside professor Alicia Arrizón explain her term "queer *mestizaje*" to a community of Mexican self-named *lesbofeministas* who completely reject the word "queer" for its Anglo-centricity, and distrust the totalizing, neo-colonial "*queerización*" of Mexican lesbian feminist genealogies? What are the ethics involved in not trying to bridge epistemological gaps between Mexican grassroots *lesbofeministas* and Mexican academic feminists with Chicana feminist theory? What do we do with *malinchismo*—a concept derived from the much-maligned historical figure of La Malinche who was given to Hernán Cortés at the time of the Spanish Conquest and who has been blamed for the downfall of the Aztec empire—as an embodied and linguistic praxis of resistance to male oppression. Or, the Chicana feminist critique and reappropriation of the Virgin of Guadalupe as both an instrument of the colonizer and a tool of indigenous liberation? How do we transinterpret the deployment of ancient Aztec mythology, particularly the myths of Coatlicue and Coyolxauhqui, as foundational stories in the grammar of Chicana feminist empowerment? What do all these terms and concepts signify in the context of US Mexican culture in general, and in the gendered experience of the authors and transinterpreters, in particular? Although some of these terms are in Spanish and the historical figures named in certain concepts originate in Mexican mythology and history, there is a particular way that Chicana theorists have appropriated those terms and given them new meanings that help us to interpret the particularities of being Mexican in the United States, of being descendants of the Treaty of Guadalupe-Hidalgo, of being constantly seen as betraying our culture, our nation and our family because of our feminism and/or lesbianism. How do we use these terms in our classrooms and in our scholarship? What is our translator's agency in the face of translation practices that privilege the academically trained rather than the empirical knowledge of Chicanas, ourselves?

Transinterpretation as the New Bridge

At the *Pocha* Poetics Seminar at UCLA in the Spring of 2014, the Codex Nepantla Collective talked at length about how to produce these "translations in the flesh," especially if some of us did not feel fluent enough in Spanish to actually translate our own work. What other method could we use if literal translation were beyond our linguistic means? Could we translate each other's work as a collective, helping each other interpret the meanings and applications of our ideas in our lived realities, and allowing those of us with more confidence or training in Spanish letters to author the work and publish it in an open-access format? Could we use art as a common language? "Transinterpretation" is the word we developed to describe the method of Chicanas translating and interpreting our own work and that of other Chicana lesbian/feminist sisters and colleagues based on affective experiential knowledge more than effective grammatical transliteration. This type of translation praxis involves not only changing words from one language to another, but also drawing on concepts, theories and images that signify Chicanx identity politics to interpret the different meanings of a text, and carrying these multiple meanings on the bridges of our backs[23] as well as our *lenguas*, our tongues and bodies. According to Webster's New World Dictionary, the word "translation" means to carry across from one place to another, to put into the words of another language or to change into another medium or form. Transinterpretation involves all three of these applications. First, transinterpretation can carry the theories, concepts and vocabularies of Chicana feminism across the border to a Mexican/Latin American/Latino audience. Second, our work can put our colonial/decolonial/postcolonial experiences and the theories by which we make sense of those experiences, historically and contemporarily, into Spanish. And third, using art as a medium of transinterpretation, we allow a visual language of symbols, icons and glyphs to communicate our *nepantlera* realities. Indeed, the scarcity of Chicana lesbian/feminist publications in Spanish, like the lack of Spanish linguistic translations and the perceived deficit of Spanish fluency among Chicana lesbian/feminist authors, raises an intertextual opportunity that makes the interpretive power of art critical to the praxis of transinterpretation. In other words, the imagery and iconography used by Chicana artists, writers and poets can function as a common language that helps to bridge linguistic and cultural divides between Chicanas and Mexicanas.[24]

Coyolteadas, or, Sneaking Chicana Lesbian/Feminist Thought South of the Border

The Codex Nepantla Collective proposes art as the conceptual *coyote* by which to smuggle Chicana lesbian/feminist thought south of the border, a type of *coyoteada* (single crossing) or *coyotaje* (tradition of crossing). Indeed, our discussion of this notion at the *Pocha* Poetics Seminar ignited a dynamic language game that produced yet another neologism, the word *coyolteada*, a theoretical diphthong that combines the notion of an unauthorized migration and the Aztec moon goddess Coyolxauhqui, the mutilated, dismembered and beheaded "bad" sister of the sun god Huitzilopochtli who tried to prevent his reign of bloodshed as the God of War and reigning deity of the Quinto Sol by killing him at the moment of his birth. Indeed, Coyolxauhqui's myth and iconography have been appropriated by Chicana lesbian feminists as a symbolic representation of the way the early *feministas* were treated and discredited by both their Chicano brothers and Chicana sisters, who judged them as lesbians (then considered an insult) and therefore as wannabe white women more concerned with promoting their own sexual interests than with supporting La Raza's revolution. The combination of these two ideas yields *coyolteada*: the unauthorized action of the "bad" sisters and daughters of the Greater Mexican nation

Figure 47. Sample Transinterpretation Postcard designed by Alma Lopez
© 2014. Used by permission of the artist.

sneaking our militant lesbian feminist discourse south of the border. Transinterpreting this idea of *coyolteadas* with her visual vocabulary, Alma created an image of a *coyota* (Chicana lesbian/
feminist and product of Mexican and American biculturality) engaging in the covert *movida* of howling her story to her sisters
south of the border with the full moon rising to the north, signifying her location in the genealogy of Coyolxauhqui.

Rather than sneaking migrants from south to north of the border, *coyolteadas* would smuggle the militant ideas of Chicana
pocha activists from north to south, a border crossing *al revés*, the
thick language of theory translated and transinterpreted by the
very authors and users of these ideas. We engage in this labor, not
because we think we are saving anybody, or because we see Mexican *lesbofeministas* and other Latina sisters as incapable of the-
orizing their own lives, but because *we* were saved by these ideas,
which, after forty years have become a legacy of *conocimiento*, a
democratic body of knowledge produced by, for and about Chi-

canas. To enact this surreptitious border-crossing *al revés*, not only must we wrestle with linguistic terrorism, colonized mind and/or *pocha* oppression, that is, discrimination enforced by our communities, our political and educational systems, our families and sometimes even ourselves, but also we must create a new Chicana lesbian/feminist vocabulary in Spanish and visual art embedded with all the layers of meaning that go into the decolonizing praxis of a thick translation.

Red Flag Translations

Gloria Anzaldúa's *Borderlands/La Frontera* (1987) and Chela Sandoval's *Methodology of the Oppressed* (2000) were the first two Chicana feminist books to be translated by the PUEG and the translations published by the UNAM in November 2015.[25] Norma Cantú and Claire Joysmith were involved in the translation of *Borderlands*, but who, I wondered, was serving as the Chicana *coyote* for *Methodology of the Oppressed*?[26] When I spoke to Chela about it and asked her if she had even given permission for her book to be translated, she said no, that because the book's copyright was in the name of the University of Minnesota Press and not the name of the author, the press had done all the negotiations with the PUEG themselves, not bothering to involve the author, to secure her permission or request her participation. I was flummoxed. By what complete self-delusion or total arrogance did the PUEG folks (by then no longer under Belausteguigoitia, I should add) think they could translate *Methodology of the Oppressed* (MotO)—a challenging text even for English-speakers—by themselves? I raised enough red flags in Chela's mind that she insisted on seeing the translation and on fixing any errors in translation that she saw. The PUEG folks agreed, but only gave her thirty days in which to make her corrections! She then enlisted the help of two of her Spanish-speaking graduate students and one of my own and requested the involvement of the Codex Nepantla team at UCLA to help evaluate the PUEG's translation of MotO.

The first problem was the title. For Chela, *Metodología de los oprimidos*, as the literal translation of the title had been rendered, was not only male-gendered, but also inaccurate, and to a certain extent condescending. She wanted to use *"metodología de la emancipación,"* since emancipation is the ultimate goal of Sandoval's decolonizing methodology, but she had to do some tedious explanation and rationalization for why the title should change so dramatically from the original. Had they actually understood MotO and the way in which the five technologies "for decolonizing the social imagination" weave together through differential social movements and oppositional consciousness to produce a single apparatus that she calls "the physics of love," they would have understood that this physics of love *is* "the apparatus of emancipation" (Sandoval 184). In other words, Chela wasn't just substituting the word *emancipación* for *los oprimidos*; she was signaling to the deepest purpose of the methodology of the oppressed: the emancipation of "citizen-subjects" from the patriarchally triangulated yoke of nationalism, imperialism and capitalism "into new, post-Western-empire alliances" (184).

Obviously, the PUEG translators didn't "get it." Just as they didn't get that "U.S. Third-World feminism" is not *"feminismo del tercer mundo,"* but rather *"feminismo tercermundista en los Estados Unidos."* In the English phrase, "U.S. Third-World" is an adjective, and feminism is the noun; hence, it is a multiracial, multicultural and multiethnic feminism developed by women of color in the United States—African Americans, Asian Americans, Chicanas, Latinas, American Indians—as a counternarrative to European or Anglo-American (or First World) feminism. In Spanish, the phrase assumes that there are two kinds of feminism, that of the First World (which the author would patently occupy as a US citizen-subject) and that of the Third World (which is her object of study). US Third-World feminism, as Chela uses it in MotO, is not feminism of the Third World, as this would imply that Chela was deploying her First World privilege to name and define a Third World experience. And the real problem here is not just that the PUEG translators didn't "get it," but more egregiously (to my eyes, anyway), that they neither sought help nor believed they needed an intervention from either the author or scholars who are more conversant with Sandoval's work. They assumed a fluent literal translation would suffice and did not seek the help of the author or of other Chicana theorists or theorists familiar with Chicana feminism because we use it in our own writings and teaching, to aid them in understanding the nuances of the text and producing the most accurate translation.[27]

In "Translation as 'Trans-Interpretation': Notes on Transforming the Book *Methodology of the Oppressed* into *Metodologia de la emancipación*," Chela Sandoval calls the Codex Nepantla Collective a "militant intellectual group . . . [of] activist-scholars" who are engaged in the "development and deployment of a method and a technique for translation we term, respectively, 'transinterpretation' and '*pocha* poetics.'"[28]

> . . . transinterpreters act as meaning-activists . . . [and] self-consciously produce revisions of language, aware that such revisions have an additional effect: They retroactively push against the very matrices of power within which an originating language is produced. Transinterpretation is thus a meta-ideological method for revision . . . [It] is a borderlands practice of re-languaging that becomes operational through "*pocha* poetics" . . . [B]y utilizing *pocha* poetics, transinterpreters create another version that repairs or returns lost, fragmented or invisible theoretical categories and/or poetic nuances. (Sandoval, "Trans-Interpretation" 27, 28)

Pocha poetics involves code-switching as a legal language of our Thirdspace[29] lives and encourages the use of our own poetic systems of syntax and vocabulary over the traditional, formal or "correct" processes of translation. For Sandoval, transinterpretation constitutes a new kind of language game. "In this game, players became re-linked to, or de-linked from their own (colonial, anti- and de-colonial) histories . . . [and] communities" (Sandoval, "Trans-Interpretation" 28). Despite all the subjectivities participating in the process, all the players in the game and all the "labyrinths of meaning" that the process of transinterpretation requires us to traverse, Sandoval acknowledges that it results in "a certain harmony comprised of a rising progression of feminist fourth-world, third-world and many-world kinships" ("Trans-Interpretation" 29). And it is this kinship that those of us engaged in the Codex Nepantla Collective want to extend to our Mexican and Latina colleagues. By engaging in writing retreats, blogging and virtual workshops via web-based video platforms; by producing a public art project of border-crossing theoretical postcards, or *coyolteadas*, that can be left in buses and metros, each bearing a Chicana feminist theory, and its literal and visual transinterpretations; and by mapping our geographical locations and creating cyberbridges between ourselves, our students and our Mexican colleagues at the UNAM and in the community, the Codex Nepantla project can help us to thick-map, thick-translate and thick-describe the Mexican metropolises on each side of the border.

Why Codex, Why Nepantla?

Borrowing the word "codex" from the name for book in Nahuatl, the Codex Nepantla collective is creating a web-based interactive multilingual "codex"—thanks to the mad skills of "digital diva," Alma Lopez—that will help to bridge the two worlds of Chicana and Mexicana feminists and to mediate the breach that exists between academic and grassroots feminists in Mexico. Bridging implies working together, coalition-building between Mexicana and Chicana feminists, and between academics and community activists, to bridge the *encrucijadas*, or crossroads, that both divide and connect us, and which include not

only linguistic and national borders—or places of friction between worlds—but also class and color differences and historically situated misconceptions of the Other. The word *nepantla*
comes from the Nahuatl, meaning "space in between." This virtual codex of Chicana lesbian/feminist theory in Spanish and visual art, we argue, can become that pedagogical Nepantla, that
"space in between" where Chicana and Mexicana feminists, lesbians and *lesbofeministas* situated along all points in the class-
and color-spectrum can initiate dialogue, compare stories, exchange ideas, raise questions, share *confianzas* and thus develop
this binational feminist "dream of a common language" (Rich
1978), a grammar of solidarity and love between women that
breaks down patriarchy, redefines power and speaks in a constantly shifting *floricanto* of poetry, art and theory.

Anzaldúa believed that it was possible for Chicanas to build
alliances not only with white feminists but also with our Mexican
and Latina academic and activist colleagues: "By highlighting
the similarities, downplaying divergences, that is, by *rapproche-
ment* between the self and the Other it is possible to build a syn-
cretic relationship. At the basis of such a relationship lies an
understanding of the effects of colonization and its resultant
pathologies" (114).[30] In other words, the internalized -isms and
phobias that infect our minds and bodies, no matter which side of
the border we're standing on, must be semiotically analyzed, the-
orized, deconstructed and re-signified in the thick layers of our
translations in the flesh, which for Mexicanas means experiencing "pedagogies of the double," or learning to see the Other (i.e.,
Chicanas) in themselves.

For Anzaldúa, "[b]ridging is the work of opening the gate to
the stranger, within and without. . . . To bridge is to attempt community, and for that we must risk being open to personal, political and spiritual intimacy, risk being wounded."[31] The work of
the Codex Nepantla Project is simply another kind of bridge, a
way of crossing over the huge chasm that separates what An-

zaldúa calls *nos/otras*, us and them, ourselves and others, who must navigate the contradictions of our world citizenships, heal the wounds of our linguistic/cultural/ differences, and find the resonances with each other's lives in our mutual Thirdspace.

> By compartiendo historias, ideas, las nepantleras forge bonds across race, gender, and other lines, thus creating a new tribalism. Este quehacer—internal work coupled with commitment to struggle for social transformation—changes your relationship to your body, and, in turn, to other bodies and to the world. And when that happens, you change the world. (Anzaldúa, "Now let us shift" 574)

Ultimately, that is the goal of the Codex Nepantla Project—to change the world, or at least to change the way that feminists and lesbians who inhabit that part of the world which incorporates Mexico and the United States and the Thirdspace in between relate, create and communicate with each other. In Alma Lopez's *Mnesic Myths* that graces the cover of this book, two female lovers occupy the Nepantla space between history and the present, between Mexican myth and Chicana art. Like these two figures, we Chicanas and Mexicanas—*lesbianas, lesbofeministas, jotas, mafloras, mariconas, tortilleras, cuirs* or whatever we call ourselves—share the blood and the cultural heritage of the indigenous people who created Coatlicue, Coyolxauhqui and la Virgen de Guadalupe. In Lopez's transinterpretation of the patriarchal myth of the volcanoes, it is not the grieving warrior Popocateptl and his suicidal lover, Ixtaccihuatl, who are the central characters of the story, but two contemporary *nepantleras*, one Chicana, one Mexicana whose embrace is imminent, and who will save each other from the violence of patriarchy, white supremacy and heteronormativity. These *nepantleras* are not grieving or killing themselves. They are, as Alma Lopez says when she talks about *Mnesic Myths*, waiting for Popocateptl to leave so they can join forces. Like Sor Juana's nocturnal warrior, or "segunda vez rebelde" from *Primero Sueño*, who loses her nightly battle with the Sun God, Helios or Huitzilopochtli, they are awaiting their chance to reassemble their severed parts and bloom again, bloom together, in the light of the Moon Goddess (see *Poems, Protest, and a Dream*, 128). They will decolonize each other with their words, their love and their lenguas.

If this is a crime, said Sor Juana, *so be it.*[32]

NOTES

Chapter 1   "Crimes of the Tongue, or, a Malinche Tree inside Me"

[1] From "Crónica mexicayotl," Nauhatl text by F. Alvarado Tezozómo in *Literatura Chicana: texto y context/Chicano Literature: Text and Context* (New York: Prentice Hall, 1972), p. xi.

[2] Carlos Fuentes, "La Herencia de La Malinche," in *ibid.*, pp. 304-306.

[3] Sandra Messinger Cypess, *La Malinche in Mexican Literature: From History to Myth* (Austin: University of Texas Press, 1991), p. 35.

[4] Adelaida Del Castillo, "Malintzin Tenepal: A Preliminary Look Into a New Perspective," in *Encuentro Femenil*, 1, 2, 58-78, 1974. The essay was reprinted under the same title in *Essays on La Mujer*, edited by Rosaura Sánchez and Rosa Martinez Cruz (Los Angeles: UCLA Chicano Studies Research Center), p. 1977. The quoted passage appears on p. 131 of that publication.

[5] See Octavio Paz, "Sons of La Malinche" in *The Labyrinth of Solitude*, translated from the Spanish by Lysander Kemp, Yara Milos, and Rachel Phillips Belash (New York: Grove Press, 1985), pp. 65-88.

[6] Cordelia Candelaria, "La Malinche, Feminist Prototype" in *Frontiers: A Journal of Women's Studies* 5, no. 2, Chicanas en el ambiente nacional/Chicanas in the National Landscape (Summer 1980): pp. 1-6.

[7] To read examples of this early Chicana poetry, see *Traitor, Survivor, Icon: The Legacy of La Malinche,* edited by Victoria I. Lyall and Terezita Romo. Denver Art Museum in association with Yale University Press, New Haven and London, 2022, pp. 166-175.

[8]Norma Alarcón, "Traddutora, Tradditora: A Paradigmatic Figure of Chicana Feminism" in *Cultural Critique* No. 13, The Construction of Gender and Modes of Social Division Issue (Autumn 1989): pp. 57-87.

[9]See Alicia Gaspar de Alba, "Malinchista: A Myth Revised" (16-17) in *Three Times a Woman: Chicana Poetry* (Tempe, AZ: Bilingual Press, 1989). Out of print. The original version of my poem, "Letters from a Bruja" in this volume does not include the names Malinal or Malintzin, just Malinche.

[10]Alicia Gaspar de Alba, "Los derechos de La Malinche," *The Mystery of Survival and Other Stories* (Tempe: Bilingual Review/ Press, 1993), pp. 47-52. Out of print. See the English version of the story, "Malinche's Rights," in this volume.

[11]Tonantzin was the honorific title for the Earth Mother, the loving goddess of life and fertility, and is associated specifically with the hill of Tepeyac where her temple once stood, the same place the Virgin of Guadalupe was said to have appeared to the Indigenous, Juan Diego in 1531, ten years after the Conquest. Indeed, scholars believe that part of the reason that the Conquest effectively converted the Native population to the Christian faith in less than a decade was that through this Virgin of Guadalupe legend, they worshipped Tonantzin in the guise of the brown Madonna. To read more about Tonantzin-Guadalupe, see Ire'ne Lara Silva's, "Goddess of the Americas in the Decolonial Imaginary: Beyond the Virtuous Virgen/Pagan Puta Dichotomy" in *Feminist Studies* 34, nos. 1 & 2 (Spring/Summer 2008), pp. 99-127. A darker aspect of Guadalupe is Coatlicue. Coatlicue, or She of the Serpent Skirt, was the fierce Mother of the Gods, whose children included Coyolxauhqui, the moon goddess, and ruling deity of the Cuarto Sol—the Sun of Peace and Abundance—and Huitzilopochtli, the sun god and the ruling deity of the Quinto Sol—the Sun of Warfare and Destruction, It was during the Quinto Sol that the Spaniards invaded their land, slaughtered them in warfare, infected them with diseases they had no immunity against, destroyed their gods and temples, raped their women, and conquered them in body and spirit. The new mestizo race (later called *la raza cósmica* by José Vasconcelos) that became the Mexican nation was born of this violent "encounter" of the two worlds.

[12]Pilar Godayol. "Malintzin/La Malinche/Doña Marina: Re-reading the Myth of the Treacherous Translator," *Journal of Iberian and Latin American Studies* 18 (2012), pp. 6-76.

[13]To read about this new mirror of *malinchismo,* see Alicia Gaspar de Alba, *Chicano Art Inside/Outside the Master's House: Cultural Politics and the CARA Exhibition* (Austin: University of Texas Press, 1998), p. 144.

Chapter 3   "Ten *Fronteriza* Meditations on La Llorona"

[1] "The Chamizal Treaty was signed August 31, 1964. The treaty granted Mexico 630 acres of what was South El Paso. September 25, 1964, Presidents Lyndon B. Johnson and Adolfo López Mateos met on the El Paso border to formally exchange the territory. The Chamizal National Memorial, marking the settlement of the U.S.-Mexico border dispute, was dedicated November 17, 1973." See "Chamizal Settlement, Freeway Bring Gigantic EP Facelifting," Sept. 25, 1964, reprinted by Trish Long in *Tales From the Morgue,* "Chamizal Treaty," May 2, 2008. Downloaded from https://www. elpasotimes.com/story/news/history/blogs/tales-from-the-morgue/2008/05/02/chamizal-treaty/31476531/ on January 18, 2021. See also James E. Hill, Jr., "El Chamizal: A Century-Old Boundary Dispute," *Geographical Review,* 55.4 (Oct. 1965), p. 518 (510-522). Downloaded from https://www.jstor.org/stable/pdf/ 212412.pdf?refreqid=excelsior%3A85522b58c1a1ecee6c73548f6e feaad3 on January 18, 2021.

[2]Most of the poems I cite in this essay were previously published in Alicia Gaspar de Alba, *La Llorona on the Longfellow Bridge: poetry y otras movidas, 1985-2001* (Houston: Arte Público Press, 2003).

Chapter 5   *Mujeres Necias*/Decolonial Feminists Unite! Dorothy Schons and Sor Juana Inés de la Cruz

[1]Sor Juana Inés de la Cruz, "Sátira filosófica" in *Obras completes de Sor Juana Inés de la Cruz I: Lírica personal,* edited by Alfonso Méndez Plancarte (Mexico: Fondo de Cultura Ecónomica, 1951, 1976, 1988), pp. 228-229. The first four lines of the poem state, "Stubborn men, who accuse/women for no reason/not seeing your-selves/as the cause of what you accuse." Translation of these lines is the author's.

[2]See Alicia Gaspar de Alba, *Sor Juana's Second Dream: A Novel* (Albuquerque: University of New Mexico Press, 1999). First edi-

tion. The novel was awarded the 2000 Latino Literary Hall of Fame Award for Best Historical Novel. It was reissued in paperback in 2007, also by University of New Mexico Press.

[3]To learn more about this mestiza, see Alicia Gaspar de Alba, *Calligraphy of the Witch: A Novel* (Houston: Arte Público Press, 2012). The first edition was published by Saint Martin's Press in 2007.

[4]See "Response to the Most Illustrious Poetess Sor Filotea de la Cruz," in *Sor Juana Inés de la Cruz: Poems, Protest, and a Dream*, translated with notes by Margaret Sayers Peden (New York: Penguin Books, 1997), pp. 1-75.

[5]This self-designation has been translated as "I, the worst of all," and is used as the title for María Luisa Bemberg's 1990 film on Sor Juana. A more literal translation would be "I, the worst [woman/nun] there has ever been, the worst in the world."

[6]Dorothy Schons, "Sor Juana: A Chronicle of Old Mexico," n.p. Dorothy Schons Papers, 1586–1955. Nettie Lee Benson Latin American Collection, University of Texas at Austin. www.lib.utexas.edu/benson.

[7]Quoted in Georgina Sabat-Rivers, "Biografías: Sor Juana vista por Dorothy Schons y Octavio Paz," *Revista Iberoamericana* 51, nos. 131-132 (July-December 1985), pp. 927-937.

[8]Interestingly, the Sor Juana Inés de la Cruz Project, a website, or "comprehensive Sor Juana online bibliography," sponsored by the Department of Spanish and Portuguese at Dartmouth College, does not include Dorothy Schons in its Bibliography of Contemporary Sor Juana scholars (nor yours truly, by the way), but it does list two books and 24 articles by Georgina Sabat de Rivers, who is called "[t]he leading Sor Juana scholar in the United States. She has dedicated her intellectual life to the study of Sor Juana's life and works. She presented her dissertation, 'El Primero sueño de Sor Juana Inés de la Cruz: tradiciones literarias y originalidad' at Johns Hopkins University in 1969." Not coincidentally, Georgina Sabat de Rivers was a student of Dorothy Schons at the University of Texas. The page was last updated on February 22, 2004. Accessed on May 29, 2020. https://www.dartmouth.edu/~sorjuana/

[9]I'm alluding here to the title of Dorothy Schons' piece, "Some Obscure Points on the Life of Sor Juana Inés de la Cruz," *Modern Philology* 24.2 (November 1926). Reprinted in *Feminist Perspectives on Sor Juana Inés de la Cruz*, edited by Stephanie Merrim (Detroit: Wayne State University Press, 1991): pp. 38–60.

[10]Octavio Paz, *Sor Juana, o Las trampas de la fe* (Barcelona: Editorial Seix Barral, 1982): p. 12.

[11]Octavio Paz, "Homenaje a Sor Juana Inés de la Cruz en su tercer centenario (1651–1695)," *Sur*, No. 206 (December 1951): pp. 29–40. Downloaded from The Sor Juana Inés de la Cruz Project at Dartmouth College on June 1, 2020. https://www.dartmouth.edu/~sorjuana/Scholars.html.

[12]Translation: "The erudite North American woman tried to understand the feminism of the poet [Sor Juana] as a reaction to Hispanic society's accentuated misogyny and closed masculine universe." This is a reference to the unpublished novel of Schons cited above, which Paz clearly read, but fails to cite in his book.

[13]Dorothy Schons, "The First Feminist in the New World," *Equal Rights,* official organ of the National Woman's Party, v.12, no.38 (Oct. 31, 1925), p. 302.

[14]Indeed, there were other publications about Sor Juana that followed Schons and preceded Paz by scholars from both sides of the border as well as from Spain, including one published in 1933 by a Mexican-American scholar, Carlos E. Castañeda, who also called Sor Juana the "first feminist of America." Nonetheless, it is Nobel laureate Octavio Paz who is credited as the ultimate authority on Sor Juana, and not an unassuming Midwestern woman who called herself Sor Juana's "rubia amiga," or blonde friend, and who made the study of Sor Juana her life's work. And there are other, mostly male, scholars who are credited with expertise about Sor Juana, among them, her biographers Diego Calleja, Fernando de la Maza, Hermilo Abreu Gómez and Alfonso Mendez Placarte. Also, writers Amado Nervo, Gabriela Mistral and Rosario Castellanos write about her as well. US-based Latin Americanists and *sorjuanistas* such as Emilie Bergmann, Amanda Powell, Stephanie Merrim and Nina Scott are some of today's most established English-language feminist interpreters of our Tenth Muse/*Décima Musa*. And, in the Spanish language, we cannot forget to include Asunción Lavrín, Mónica

Lavín and Sara Poot Herrera among the long list of *sorjuanistas*. Nowadays, plenty of popular sources abound as well. YouTube alone is filled with all manner of videos on Sor Juana's life from all over the world, created by a range of Sor Juana aficionados—students, scholars, filmmakers, writers, musicians and meme-makers.

[15]Guillermo Schmidhuber de la Mora, *Dorothy Schons: La primera sorjuanista, con la colaboración de Olga Martha Peña Doria* (Buenos Aires, Argentina: Editorial Dunken, 2012). Author's translation. Original: *"acaso porque sus profesores infravaloraban que una mujer investigara a otra mujer en un tiempo en que la figura humana y literaria de Sor Juana no había sido consolidada."* De la Mora observes that, while Schons' first articles on Sor Juana had been published in the mid- to late 1920s, it was not until 1934 that she returned to her Sor Juana scholarship to debunk the notion of some Catholic critics that Sor Juana had somehow given up her studies and "found religion" at the time of her death.

[16]Her death certificate cites "a self-inflicted gunshot wound" due to her "extreme nervous condition becoming worse," saying her body was discovered with "a 32 cal. pistol [placed] at the head." See *"Acta de difunción de* Dorothy Schons" in the Dorothy Schons Papers, and in Schmidhuber de la Mora, *Dorothy Schons: La primera sorjuanista*, p. 14.

[17]Guillermo Schmidhuber de la Mora, *La secreta amistad de Juana y Dorotea: obra de teatro en siete escenas* (México: Instituto Mexiquense de Cultura, 1999), p. 19.

[18]Emma Pérez, *The Decolonial Imaginary: Writing Chicanas into History* (Bloomington: Indiana University Press, 1999): p. xv.

[19]I'm paraphrasing Paz's argument here. See *Las trampas de la fe*, p. 14.

[20]Georgina Sabat de Rivers, *En busca de Sor Juana* (Mexico City: UNAM, facultad de filosofía y letras, 1998), p. 50. Author's translation: "Our Sor Juana of the seventeenth century was that revolutionary woman for whose existence we find glimmers in today's feminist criticism."

[21]Sor Juana Inés de la Cruz, "Quéjase de la suerte: insinúa su aversión a los vicios, y justifica su divertimiento a las Musas," or "She Complains Of Her Fate: Insinuates Her Aversion to Vices, and Justifies Her Diversion to the Muses." Translation by the author. For

the full text of the original poem and its English translation, see Sayers Peden, *Protest and a Dream*, p. 170.

[22]I am summarizing two of Sor Juana's poems here, "She Assures that She Will Hold a Secret in Confidence," in *Sor Juana Inés de la Cruz: Poems: A Bilingual Anthology*, translated by Margaret Sayers Peden (Tempe, AZ: Bilingual Press, 1985), p. 45; and "Excusing herself for silence, on being summoned to break it" in *A Sor Juana Anthology*, translated by Alan Trueblood, Foreword by Octavio Paz (Cambridge: Harvard University Press, 1988), p. 43.

[23]See Emma Pérez, "Sexuality and Discourse: Notes of a Chicana Survivor," in *Chicana Lesbians: The Girls Our Mothers Warned Us About*, edited by Carla Trujillo (Berkeley: Third Woman Press, 1991), pp. 159-184.

[24]The full title of the book is *Inundación castálida de la única poetisa, musa décima, Soror Juana Inés de la Cruz, Religiosa professa en el Monasterio de San Gerónimo de la Imperial Ciudad de México. Que en varios metros, idiomas, y estilos fertiliza varios assumptos; con elegantes, sutiles, claros, ingeniosos, útiles versos: para enseñanza, recreo, y admiración*. Madrid: Juan García Infanzón, 1689. Author's translation: Castalian inundation of the only poetess, tenth muse, Sor Juana Inés de la Cruz, a professed nun in the Monastery of Saint Jerome of the Imperial City of Mexico. That in various meters, languages and styles fertilizes several matters: with elegant, subtle, clear, ingenious and useful verses: for teaching, recreation and admiration. The epithet, *décima musa*, is a play on words that has a double meaning. It refers to Sor Juana as a muse of the *décima*, a popular poetic form of the Spanish Golden Age, and it compares Sor Juana's poetic skills (and perhaps her same-sex desires) to those of Sappho.

[25]"Hear me with your eyes," a line from Sor Juana Inés de la Cruz, Sonnet 211, titled "Que expresan sentimientos de ausente," in *A Sor Juana Anthology*, translated by Alan S. Trueblood (Cambridge: Harvard University Press, 1988), p. 70.

[26]See Alicia Gaspar de Alba, "The Sor Juana Chronicles" in *[Un]Framing the "Bad Woman: Sor Juana, Malinche, Coyolxauhqui and Other Rebels With a Cause*. Austin: University of Texas Press, 2014, 268. Also see "The Politics of Location of *La*

Décima Musa: Prelude to an Interview" and "Interview with Sor Juana Inés de la Cruz" in the same volume.

Chapter 7   *"Ella Tiene Su Tono"*: Conocimiento and Mestiza Consciousness in Liliana Wilson's Art

[1] Gloria Anzaldúa, *Borderlands/La Frontera: The New Mestiza* (San Francisco: Aunt Lute Press, 1987). The book is now in its 5th edition.

[2] Gloria Anzaldúa, "Now let us shift . . . the path of conocimiento . . . inner work, public acts," in *This Bridge We Call Home: Radical Visions for Transformation*, edited by Gloria Anzaldúa and Ana Louise Keating (New York: Routledge, 2002), p. 544.

[3] Adrienne Rich, *The Dream of a Common Language: Poems, 1974-1977* (New York: Norton & Co., 1978).

[4] Anzaldúa described *Nepantla* as "an in-between state, that uncertain terrain one crosses when moving from one place to another." Anzaldúa explains in her Preface to *This Bridge We Call Home* (2002) that she uses the concept of Nepantla to "theorize liminality and to talk about those who facilitate passages between worlds." For Anzaldúa, Nepantla is associated "with states of mind that question old ideas and beliefs, acquire new perspectives, change worldviews, and shift from one world to another" (Preface, 1).

[5] Liliana Wilson, email to the author, September 16, 2008.

[6] Gloria Anzaldúa, "Bearing Witness: Their Eyes Anticipate the Healing," in *Tongues* 3 (2003): pp. 34-35.

[7] Liliana Wilson, personal interview, March 22, 2008, Austin, Texas.

[8] The nine demons in this image reminded me of the 9 circles of Hell in Dante's Inferno. Dante and his spiritual guide, Virgil descend into each circle so that Dante can see what awaits the soul of one who renounces the Christian God, each level taking him further down into the bowels of the earth, where Satan lives. Shaped like a spiraling funnel, Hell consists of the following levels: Limbo, place of the Virtuous Pagans who were born prior to Christianity; the Lustful, the Gluttonous; the Hoarders and Wasters, the Wrathful, the Heretics, the Violent, the Fraudulent and the Treacherous.

[9] *La facultad* does not just occur in margin-dwellers in the United States. Any social, racial, sexual, linguistic, religious "minority"

(despite actual demographics) that differs from the patriarchal ruling paradigm can be said to have *facultad.*

[10]Anzaldúa shows how the militaristic, male-dominated Aztecs/Mexica had already started this process of trampling the feminine even before the Christian *conquistadores* set foot on Mexican shores and completed the job. It was the cult of Huitzilopochtli, the God of War, that "drove the powerful female deities underground by giving them monstrous attributes and by substituting male deities in their place, thus splitting the female Self and the female deities. They divided her who had been complete, who possessed both upper (light) and underworld (dark) aspects" (*Borderlands* p. 49).

[11]Liliana Wilson, telephone interview, September 29, 2008.

[12]The online Wiktionary explains that "crisis" comes "from the ancient Greek κρίσις (krisis) 'a separating, power of distinguishing, decision, choice, election, judgment, dispute' < κρίνω (krino) 'to pick out, to choose, to decide, to judge.'" Thus, a crisis is a turning point, a crucial and decisive situation. http://xmlgadgets.com/home.pl?site=mwikt&query=crisis.

[13]http://en.wikipedia.org/wiki/Crisis Accessed 9/28/08.

[14]*Pocho/pocha* is a derogatory term that signifies someone who speaks a botched Spanish. It is used by cultural purists in Mexico who believe Chicanas/os are corrupting the Spanish language by mixing it with English, and who see this form of speaking as a sign of betrayal to the homeland, or mother culture.

[15]Julie Reynolds, "The Nepantla Experiment," *El Andar Magazine* (November 1995). Back issue accessed online at http://www.elandar.com/back/www-nov95/feature/feature.htm.

[16]After launching an insurgent uprising on January 1, 1994, the Ejército Zapatista de Liberación Nacional (EZLN) in Chiapas was declared in a state of war against the Mexican state. The Mexican military was deployed into Chiapas to squelch the uprising, killing thousands of indigenous "insurgents" and civilians, and pushing the base of the EZLN forces into the Lacandon Jungle. There is a coincidental link between the date of the uprising and the date that NAFTA, the North American Free Trade Agreement, was implemented.

[17]In this chapter of *Borderlands*, "Tlilli, Tlapalli/The Path of the Red and Black Ink," Anzaldúa talks about how using the actual [black] ink of her pen to write down the stories of the red [pain] she carries in her blood, sometimes makes her physically ill. "Because writing invokes images from my unconscious and because some of the images have residues of trauma which I then have to reconstruct, I sometimes get sick when I do write. I can't stomach it, become nauseous, or burn with fever, worsen. But in reconstructing the traumas behind the images, I make 'sense' of them, and once they have 'meaning' they are changed, transformed. It is then that writing heals me, brings me great joy" (92).

[18]Chela Sandoval, *Methodology of the Oppressed* (Minneapolis: University of Minnesota Press, 1999), p. 141.

[19]See José Vasconcelos, *La raza cósmica/The cosmic race*, a bilingual edition (Baltimore: Johns Hopkins University Press, 1979). For as seminal (I use the word on purpose) as the Vasconcelan notion of a cosmic race became with Raza activists in the Chicano Movement of the 1960s and 1970s, his thesis is fundamentally flawed. Rather than a theory of racial liberation, it is instead a treatise on New World eugenics riddled with racist stereotypes: the Chinese, he writes, "under the saintly guidance of Confucian morality multiply like mice" (19); "the Black, eager for sensual joy, intoxicated with dances and unbridled lust"; "the Mongol, with the mystery of his slanted eyes that see everything according to a strange angle"; or the Anglos, with their "clear vision of a great destiny . . . the intuition of a definite historical mission" whose imperial cause is guided "by God himself" and whose blood is not tainted "by the contradictory instincts of a mixture of dissimilar races" (17). Indeed, that is the true message of Vasconcelos' "*raza cósmica*," not the celebration of *mestizaje*, per se, but the pursuit of a perfect race, a new race composed of a mixture of similar races, made more and more dissimilar, and yet with more of the strong traits of the white race, through the process of miscegenation. If Chicano/a activists had really read the full text of our illustrious Vasconcelos, they would have found his analysis of how Mexicans came to be, not by rape and conquest, but rather by "that abundance of love that allowed the Spaniard to create a new race with the Indian and the Black, profusely spreading white ancestry

through the soldier who begat a native family" (17). Thus the purpose of mixing the races is to strengthen and purify, that is, whiten, the blood more and more until finally, "[w]hat is going to emerge out there is the definitive race, the synthetical race, the integral race, made up of the genius and the blood of all peoples and, for that reason, more capable of a true brotherhood and of a truly universal vision" (20). I think this was the only utopian sentence Chicano/a activists actually read.

Chapter 8   "Bad Girls Rise Again: The *Sinful Saints & Saintly Sinners at the Margins of the Americas* Exhibition"

[1]Article accessed on July 7, 2013, at http://www.sfreporter.com/santafe/article-7526 shame-as-it-ever-was.html.
[2]The official canonized patron saint of Mexican immigrants is Saint Toribio, a Jalisco priest named Father Toribio Romo González who was martyred during Mexico's Cristero War (1926-29).
[3]The other pieces in the series are titled *California Fashion Slaves, 187, La Línea* and *Santa Niña de Mochis*.
[4]The Treaty of Guadalupe Hidalgo ceded over 50 percent of Mexico's territory to the United States after Mexico lost the US-Mexico War (1846-1848). Over 100,000 Mexicans lost their land as well as their citizenship because of the Anglo takeover of northern Mexico that became spoils of war in the Treaty.
[5]*Our Lady de Coyolxauhqui* is a new print featuring Lopez's *Our Lady of Controversy* wearing boxing gloves with a Coyolxauhqui halo rising behind her. Lopez's screen printed this image on eighteen first edition hardcover copies of the book *Our Lady of Controversy: Alma López's "Irreverent Apparition,"* (2011).
[6]The term *pocho* refers to Mexican-origin people in the United States, typically second-, third- and fourth generation, who are English-dominant, and, either speak no Spanish, or speak Spanglish more comfortably than Spanish. For Mexican nationals, *pochos* and *pochas* are seen in a derogatory light, as traitors to the Mexican homeland.
[7]Heather Levi, *The World of Lucha Libre: Secrets, Revelations, and Mexican National Identity* (Durham: Duke University Press, 2008), p. 105. All the quotes here are taken from the same page.

[8]Perhaps this is why Alma Lopez's *Our Lady* has the power to shock more than any of her other Guadalupana images, precisely because, as Judithe Hernández notes, in reverse, "the [more] realistic the image, the [more] sexualized the interpretation of the female form." [9]The Penitente Brotherhood, also known as Los Hermanos, is a Christian cult of flagellants in northern New Mexico dedicated to emulating the penance and passion of Christ. They live ascetic lives, gather for worship in remote meeting houses in the mountains and hold processions during Holy Week that reenact the Crucifixion.

Chapter 10   "The Codex Nepantla Project: TransInterpretation as Pocha Poetics, Politics, and Praxis"

[1]LesVoz, cofounded by Mariana Pérez Ocaña and Juana Guzmán, is best known as the publisher of the first lesbian literary magazine in Mexico and producer of six mammoth lesbian marches in Mexico City (*Marcha Lésbica*). "*Semana Cultural*" is one of its more recent cultural interventions, bringing lesbian cultural production from throughout Mexico and the United States into community spaces. [2]To respect the privacy of the participants, many of whom were fighting in their own communities and families against physical violence for their lesbianism and harassment for their radical feminist politics, they are not named here. In sum, a strong contingent of the group viewed queer theory as white, socially privileged and male-dominant. That queer theory had become so popular in the Mexican academy clearly spoke to them about the colonizing tendency of white male discourse, which they felt was erasing the history of Mexican feminism and particularly the *lesbofeminista* movement. Alma and I tried to explain the difference between this totalizing kind of queer theory, which was also becoming a dominating discourse in the US academy, and the particular ways in which queers and trans folks of color have appropriated but also changed the term to QTPOC (queer trans people of color) theory to signify their intersectional oppressions within that dominant white male discourse, but the *lesbofeminista* animosity against all things "*cuir*" did not permit another reading. [3]In *Beyond the Pink Tide*, Macarena Gómez-Baris defines "*lo cuir*" not as an embracement of queer theory or identity as these are con-

structed in the Anglophone world, but instead as an interpretation of the untranslatable re-semanticization, or pride of sexual difference, embedded in the word "queer," whose literal translation in Spanish would be "*raro*," which means not rare, as in highly valuable, but strange as in colonizing. To differentiate between the decolonial and the colonial interpretations of the term, the English word "queer" becomes Hispanicized to the phonetic "*cuir*," which Gómez-Baris reminds us, is "located within deeper histories of colonial exchange" in the Americas that "account for sexual difference in their specific geopolitical context" from the northern borders of Mexico to the southern tip of Argentina" (*Beyond the Pink Tide: Art and Political Undercurrents in the Americas*. Berkeley: University of California Press, 2018, 57). Gómez-Baris rejects the notion of one overarching notion of "*lo cuir*" in Latin America, but acknowledges that "*[l]o cuir*, then, becomes a powerful mode of embodied political activity that is not merely the result of US imperialism, but names relational viewpoints from throughout the Southern Hemisphere" (57-58). For the *lesbofeministas* of LesVoz, however, *lo cuir* is simply a linguistic substitute for the colonizing Anglo term "queer," a theory and practice that feels entitled to taking up space and demanding accommodation in all gender-based movements.

[4]Respectively, the National Association of Chicano Studies (NACS), created in 1972, which twenty years later changed its acronym to NACCS, or the National Association of Chicana and Chicano Studies; in 1982, Chicana feminists created MALCS, or *Mujeres Activas en Letras y Cambio Social*, as a form of protest against Chicano sexism in NACS.

[5]The *Joto* Caucus also saw the need to expand their membership to include Bisexual and Trans folks, but for some reason, they did not alter the name of the caucus to reflect the new membership and were able to retain their "*joto*," or gay male nomenclature. Perhaps they were not pressured from within to make this change, or a vote was taken and those voting for *Joto* Caucus prevailed.

[6]Luminaries of Chicanx *belles lettres* include John Rechy, Sandra Cisneros, Ana Castillo, Helena María Viramontes, Reyna Grande, Luis Alberto Urrea and Benjamin Alire Saenz.

[7]This is not to say that there are no Chicanas writing in Spanish or translating their own work. Author and editor, Norma Cantú, cur-

rently Murchison Professor in the Humanities at Trinity University in San Antonio, who is also professor emeritus of the University of Texas, San Antonio and founder of the Society for the Study of Gloria Anzaldúa, has been at the forefront of translating Chicana feminist thought, particularly the work of Gloria Anzaldúa; indeed, her translation of *Borderlands/La Frontera* was one of the two Chicana lesbian/feminist titles published by the PUEG in 2015. On a more personal note, I have transinterpreted my own work, both poetry and prose, since my graduate school days in the early 1980s, and several of my self-translations have been published in Mexico.

[8] Elena Poniatowska, "Chicanas y Mexicanas," *MELUS: Other Americas* 21 (3): pp. 35-51.

[9] Since *"historia"* in Spanish means both history and fiction, a literal translation of the terms would be "self-story/self-history" and "self-story/self-history-theory." Although she expounded this method of self-writing, and practiced it throughout her oeuvre, including her poetry, Anzaldúa did not actually define these terms until 2002, in a footnote to her "now let us shift" essay in *This Bridge We Call Home*. *"Autohistoria* is a term I use to describe the genre of writing about one's personal and collective history using fictive elements, a sort of fictionalized autobiography or memoir; an *autohistoria-teoría* is a personal essay that theorizes" (578).

[10] Codex Nepantla has a three-fold mission: 1) to change Chicana lesbian/feminist theory from English to Spanish, 2) to create a Chicana lesbian/feminist vocabulary in Spanish for foundational terminology and 3) to use visual art to interpret Chicana lesbian/feminist theories and concepts with the aid of cultural iconography—all of which constitute the Nepantla process that we call transinterpretation, which is at once a decolonial pedagogy, a praxis in genuine respect for the Other, and a tool for social change.

[11] A *nepantlera* is Anzaldúa's new mestiza who fully inhabits the ambivalent, contradictory in-between third space or third culture between two or more critical realities, be they national identities, languages, genders, sexualities, world views and/or spiritualities.

[12] The lack of research funding has also been a roadblock to the project. From 2012-2017, I applied broadly for inter- and intra-mural grants to support Codex Nepantla (including a UC MEXUS-CONACYT Collaborative grant between the department of Chi-

cana/o Studies at UCLA and the Program of Gender Studies at the UNAM), but my proposal has been turned down because, instead of a research-based endeavor, the project is seen as "just translation." To date, the only funding the project has received is the University of California Humanities Research Institute Seminar Grant in the amount of $4000 for the "*Pocha* Poetics" seminar at UCLA.

[13]Names and affiliations of the faculty participants: UC Santa Barbara: Chela Sandoval and Ellie Hernández; UC Riverside: Alicia Arrizón and Tiffany López; Loyola Marymount University: Deena González; UCLA: Alma Lopez and Alicia Gaspar de Alba; and Italian professor Paola Zaccaria who has published extensively on translating Gloria Anzaldúa and who happened to be visiting *Profesora* Sandoval at Santa Barbara. The rest of the participant/attendees were graduate students from the same UC campuses attending with their mentors. Go to https://lgbtqstudies.ucla.edu/photos/pocha-poetics-2014/ to see pictures of the event.

[14]Walter Benjamin, "The Task of the Translator" in *Illuminations*, edited by Hannah Arendt. Translated by Harry Zohn. New York: Schocken Books, 1969, pp. 69-82.

[15]Kwame Anthony Appiah, "Thick Translation," *Callaloo*. 16.4 (1993): pp. 808-819.

[16]Gloria Anzaldúa, *Gloria Anzaldúa: Interviews/Entrevistas*, edited by AnaLouise Keating. New York: Routledge, 2000.

[17]Clifford Geertz, "Thick Description: Toward an Interpretive Theory of Culture" in *The Interpretation of Cultures: Selected Essays*. New York: Basic Books, 1973, pp. 3-30.

[18]Lawrence Venuti, *The Translator's Invisibility: A History of Translation*, 2nd edition. New York: Routledge, 1995.

[19]With the exception of Norma Cantú, who is the named translator of the PUEG's first edition translation of *Borderlands/La Frontera: La Nueva Mestiza* in 2015. At the time of the formation of Codex Nepantla, however, that translation had still not been published.

[20]Norma Klahn, "Literary (Re)Mappings: Autobiographical (Dis)-Placements by Chicana Writers," in Gabriela F. Arredondo, et.al. (eds.), *Chicana Feminisms: A Critical Reader* (Durham, N.C.: Duke University Press), p. 138.

[21]Claire Joysmith, "De espejos, cantares y cruces: a manera de introducción," *Cantares de espejos: poesía testimonial chicana de mujeres* (Mexico City: Centro de Investigaciones sobre América del Norte/Universidad del Claustro de Sor Juana, 2012), p. 26.

[22]Marisa Belausteguigoitia and Maria del Socorro Gutiérrez Magallanes, "Chicana/o and Latina/o Literary Studies in Mexico," in *The Routledge Companion to Latino/a Literature*, edited by Suzanne Bost and Frances Aparicio. New York: Routledge, 95-106.

[23]Here, I am alluding to the title of the first of the transformative Chicana lesbian feminist anthologies, *This Bridge Called My Back: Writings by Radical Women of Color*, co-edited by Gloria Anzaldúa and Cherríe Moraga. New York: Kitchen Table: Women of Color Press, 1981.

[24]For more about this method of translation and its uses in bridging the worlds of Chicana and Mexicana lesbian feminists, check out our collective blog, www.codexnepantla.net.

[25]Anzaldúa's translation was published on Nov. 18, 2015, and Sandoval's on Nov. 25, 2015, a week apart. For reasons unknown to me, Joysmith wanted her name removed from the project, although she was the translator of the poetry section of *Borderlands*.

[26]Chela Sandoval, *Methodology of the Oppressed*. Minneapolis: University of Minnesota Press, 2000.

[27]Sandoval's experience with transinterpretation is more than theoretical, for she got to practice and see the results of the method in the Collective's interventions with some of the rewritings and resignifications of the "official" Spanish translation produced by the Mexican translator contracted by the PUEG without any idea of the thick layers of context and meaning embedded in the original.

[28]Chela Sandoval, "Translation as Trans-Interpretation: Notes on Transforming the Book *Methodology of the Oppressed* into *Metodología de la emancipación*," in *Chicana/Latina Studies*, vol. 17, issue 2 (Spring 2018): pp. 26-32.

[29]See Homi Bhabha, *The Location of Culture*. New York: Routledge, 1994. Bhabha stresses the necessity for colonized cultures to translate and negotiate their cultural identities within discourses of cultural difference enunciated as cultural hybridity. He theorizes the Thirdspace as "enunciations" of "cultural difference," in which "we may elude the politics of polarity and emerge as the others of our

selves" (39). Within Chicana discourse, Chela Sandoval, Emma Pérez, Norma Alarcón and Gloria Anzaldúa have all written about this Thirdspace, or space in-between two worlds, whether that applies culturally, linguistically or in terms of the nation-state. Thirdspace feminism, for example, is that space in between mainstream white feminism with its emphasis on gender oppression and power inequalities within patriarchy and Third World feminism, a decolonial feminist praxis articulated by women of color with cultural and linguistic roots in the colonized Third World that intersects sexism with racism, classism, settler colonialism, heterosexism, xenophobia and homophobia. In *The Decolonial Imaginary*, Emma Pérez argues "that the differential mode of consciousness to which [Chela] Sandoval refers [in her essay "U.S. Third World Feminism"] is precisely third space feminist practice, and that practice can occur only within the decolonial imaginary," since both concepts are "theoretical tool[s] for uncovering the hidden voices of Chicanas that have been relegated to silences, to passivity, to that third space where agency is enacted through third space feminism" (xvi).

[30]Gloria Anzaldúa, "En Rapport, In Opposition: Cobrando cuentas a las nuestras," in *The Gloria Anzaldúa Reader*, edited by AnaLouise Keating. Durham: Duke University Press, 2009, pp. 111-118.

[31]Gloria Anzaldúa, "(Un)natural bridges, (un)safe spaces," in *The Gloria Anzaldúa Reader*, p. 246.

[32]Sor Juana Inés de la Cruz, poem 56, in *A Sor Juana Anthology*, Translated by Alan S. Trueblood, Foreword by Octavio Paz. Cambridge: Harvard University Press, 1988, p. 88. The translation of Sor Juana's lines, "*Si es delito, ya lo digo;/si es culpa, ya la confieso*" is the author's.

ACKNOWLEDGEMENTS

This is my 13th book. People ask me what's the secret to my productivity, and I always say, not sleeping. This is not an exaggeration. It's not possible to juggle a full-time, full-blast academic career at UCLA and a successful creative writing career and be able to sleep a normal amount of hours. My normal, in terms of sleep, averages to about 4 hours a night, although some nights, it's no more than two, and other nights, especially at deadline time, none at all. So yes, not sleeping has carved out the space for me to work long past the midnight hour, burning all my candles on both ends, to produce and produce and produce. Through it all, over the last 14 years, my darling, my wife, Alma Lopez, despite her own difficulties with her health, and her own challenges with balancing an artistic career with the demands of family life and academia, has supported me, encouraged me and taken care of me, and even, put up with an empty bed night after night after night. Most partners would not tolerate so much absence, and some might even feel abandoned and resentful while I sit in the next room madly working my fingers over the keyboard till the wee hours. But not Alma, because she's an artist and she knows how important it is to be able to work on one's art. And because she's Alma, and she loves me. And this, really, is the secret to my productivity, the stability of this love, the generosity, the kindness, the patience. True to her name, Alma is also my inspiration, and I thank her for her brilliant art that graces the covers of my books and that gives me so much to contemplate in my work. Thank you to our daughter, Azul, who daily asks me to dance with her and challenges me to be the best Mapi I can be. Thank you to my mom, Teyali Falcón, for trusting me with her story; I hope I have done it justice as I wove it into my own. Thank you to my familia of friends who over the last three decades have become integral to the homebase of my life, whose work has always inspired me, and who have shared adventures, advice and necessary admonitions over the years: Emma Pérez, Deena González, Teresa Córdova, Liliana Wilson, Cynthia Pérez, Dina Flores, Antonia Castañeda, Arturo Madrid and Tomás Ybarra-Frausto. To my colleagues, Charlene Villaseñor Black and Mitchell Morris for your support and example. To Patrick Polk and Marla Berns of the Fowler Museum for integrating my work into the cultural fabric of UCLA. To the Codex Nepantla Collective, especially everyone who attended the *Pocha* Poetics Seminar, and who contributed their time, insights and experiences to the theory and praxis of transinterpretation: Chela Sandoval, Alicia Arizona, Tiffany López, Maria Cristina Pons, Kendy Rivera, Max Greenberg, Sandra Ruiz, Elena Aviles, and to Mariana Ocaña Pérez, Yan María Castro y las compañeras de Les-Voz for motivating this linguistic quest. To the Queen of Spades and the Queen of Clubs of our poker club, Lindsey Haley and Ayde González, for all the laughter and good fun. To Azul's madrinas, who made it possible for Alma and me to escape on date nights at critical times during the writing of these pieces: Sombra Ruiz, Deborah Hall and FaFa Collins. And to the memory of my muy querida comadre, Blanca Gaspar de Alba, who never failed to buy my books and share my work with her friends. Thank you, Comadre, for being my "number-one fan."

Finally, I also want to acknowledge the editors and publishers who have helped bring my books to life since 1993: Gary Keller at Bilingual Press, Theresa May at the University of Texas Press and, of course, Nicolás Kanellos and his indefatigable staff, especially Marina Tristán and Gabriela Baeza Ventura at Arte Público Press.

Most of the essays and stories in this collection are revised and expanded versions of previously published pieces. All were updated in 2022.

1. A slightly different version of "Crimes of the Tongue: A Malinche Tree Inside Me" was published in *Traitor, Survivor, Icon: The Legacy of La Malinche*, exhibition catalogue, edited by Victoria I. Lyall and Terezita Romo, Denver: Yale University Press, 2022.
2. "Ten Fronteriza Meditations on La Llorona" was invited for and is forthcoming in *Weeping Women: La Llorona's Presence in Modern Latinx and Chicanx Lore,* an Anthology, edited by Kathleen Alcalá and Norma E. Cantú, with a Preface by Domino Renée Pérez. San Antonio: Trinity University Press.
3. A slightly different version of *"Ella tiene su tono*: Mestiza Consciousness and Conocimiento in Liliana Wilson's Art" was previously published in *Ofrenda: Liliana Wilson's Art of Dissidence and Dreams*, edited by Norma E. Cantú. College Station, TX: Texas A&M Press, 2015, pp. 53-68.
4. "Bad Girls Rise Again" was previously published as "Bad Girls on the Rise" in *Sinful Saints & Saintly Sinners at the Margins of the Americas*, exhibition catalogue, edited by Patrick A. Polk. Los Angeles: Fowler Museum at UCLA, pp. 139-151.
5. "Mujeres Necias/Decolonial Feminists Unite! Dorothy Schons and Sor Juana Inés de la Cruz" is an edited and revised combination of two previously published pieces: "Decolonial Feminists Unite: Dorothy Schons and Sor Juana Inés de la Cruz" published in *Portal: A Centennial Celebration of the Nettie Lee Benson Latin American Collection.* Issue No. 15. 2019-2020, pp. 22-29 and "Sor Juana Inés de la Cruz" published in *Revolutionary Women of Texas and Mexico: Portraits of Soldaderas, Saints, and Subversives*, edited by Kathy Sosa, Ellen Riojas Clark, and Jennifer Speed, with a Foreword by Dolores Huerta and an Afterword by Norma Elia Cantú. San Antonio: Trinity University Press, 2020, pp. 105-117.
6. An earlier version of "The Codex Nepantla Project: Transinterpretation as Pocha Poetics, Politics, and Praxis" was published in *Chicana/Latina Studies: The Journal of Mujeres Activas en Letras y Cambio Social.* Volume 20, Issue 2. Spring 2021: pp. 96-120.

7. "The Border Beat, 1921" is a revised version of "American Citizen, 1921," originally published in *The Mystery of Survival and Other Stories*. Tempe, AZ: Bilingual Press, 1993. Out of print.

8. "The Mystery of Survival" is a revised version of a story by the same title published originally in *ibid*.

9. "The Piñata Dream" is a revised version of a story by the same title published originally in *ibid*.

10. "Malinche's Rights is a translated and revised version of the story "Los derechos de La Malinche," originally published in *ibid*. An earlier version of the English translation was published in *Currents from a Dancing River: Contemporary Latino Fiction, Nonfiction, and Poetry* edited by Ray González. New York: Harcourt Brace, 1994, pp. 261-266.